The Healthy Slow Cooker Cookbook

THE Healthy Slow Cooker Cookbook

*150 Fix-and-Forget Recipes
Using Delicious,
Whole-Food Ingredients*

ROCKRIDGE
PRESS

At a Glance

This book will provide the inspiration and recipes to help you create delicious, satisfying, and healthy meals for your family with the ease and convenience of a slow cooker. All the recipes in this cookbook have been developed to fulfill the following requirements:

Dishes feature healthy, accessible, whole-food ingredients so you can avoid processed foods, trans fats, and artificial sweeteners.

Meals involve minimal preparation, typically less than 15 minutes, and require no stirring or adding ingredients midway through the cooking process (with exceptions for delicate ingredients like certain seafood or leafy vegetables, which are added within the final half hour of cooking).

Dietary labels are used to designate which recipes are vegan, vegetarian, gluten-free, or Paleo-friendly (no grains, dairy, legumes, processed sugars, or white potatoes).

Nutritional information is provided to help you keep track of the calories, fat, protein, carbs, sugar, and sodium you consume.

Contents

INTRODUCTION

■ ■ ■ ■ ■ ■ ■ ■ ■ ■ ■ ■ ■ ■ ■ ■ ■ ■ ■ ■

Possibly the only thing better than sharing a delicious meal with the people you love is being able to slow down and prepare that meal in a calm and relaxed manner. A slow cooker provides a convenient opportunity to do both. Bonus: A slow cooker also requires very little cleanup (everything is prepared in one dish), leaving you with even more time for enjoyment.

Although cooking with a slow cooker is a convenient—even nostalgic—option for busy people, many slow cooker cookbooks rely on processed foods such as canned soups, frozen prepared meats, or packaged salad dressings, which are not very appetizing or healthy. It doesn't have to be this way!

With this book you can say *sayonara* to prepared mixes and canned soup in favor of fresh, whole-food ingredients. You can say *adios* to stirring throughout cooking or adding ingredients at various stages. You simply prepare the food, put it into the slow cooker, cover, and then sit back and look forward to a delicious meal.

The recipes in this book are designed to please the palates of children and adults alike. You'll find delicious twists on classic American favorites, such as Sage and Pumpkin Mac 'n' Cheese (page 86) and Sweet Potato Pudding (page 55), as well as exotic dishes, such as Indian Chickpeas with Yogurt and Cardamom (page 106), Mussels in Saffron Curry Broth (page 117), and Thai Sweet and Sour Soup (page 43). You'll also find ingredient variations if you wish to further reduce sodium, fat, or sugar.

Explore the wide range of simple yet enticing recipes, from breakfasts to appetizers and soups to hearty main dishes, and enjoy the extra time this style of cooking will afford you.

Healthy Slow Cooking

■ ■ ■ ■ ■ ■ ■ ■ ■ ■ ■ ■ ■ ■ ■ ■ ■

Nourishing the people you love—including yourself—with healthful foods is one of the greatest gifts you can give. It provides immediate nutritional benefits and can help form a lifetime of positive eating habits and vibrant health.

According to the Mayo Clinic, a healthy diet should include a variety of foods from all the major food groups, including plenty of fresh produce; whole grains; dairy; lean protein from meat, fish, beans, and legumes; as well as nuts, seeds, and healthy fats. The organization also recommends choosing foods you can afford and that fit your tastes; it's not sustainable if you spend your entire paycheck on expensive organic produce or force yourself to eat healthy foods you don't like. Palatability may not seem so important for health, but the more flavorful and enjoyable you find healthy foods, the more likely you are to include them in your menu.

Achieving all of this in the midst of demanding jobs and busy schedules isn't so easy. Pulling together a nutritionally balanced meal after a long day can be tough. That's where a slow cooker can help!

THE BENEFITS OF SLOW COOKING

Cooking food in a slow cooker provides numerous benefits over other cooking methods.

- In addition to producing great-tasting food, a slow cooker offers the ultimate in convenience cooking. You can prepare your ingredients in advance, mix them in your slow cooker, turn it on, and come home to a hot, delicious, and nutritious meal.

- The slow cooker yields a moisture-rich cooking environment, so less oil is needed to prevent sticking or burning. Less oil means fewer calories. It also reduces the opportunity for oxidation to occur—and thus preventing the formation of free radicals and harmful compounds—when cooking oils such as vegetable oil and canola oil are heated for long periods of time. (When added fats are necessary to a recipe, we recommend using heat-stable fats such as butter and coconut oil.)

- Slow cooker meals are usually one-dish meals that utilize the resulting sauces and cooking liquids, so more of the nutrients remain in the dish.

- Slow cooking at low heat is less likely to expose you to advanced glycation end products, or AGEs, which are toxins our bodies absorb from fried, grilled, or broiled foods. AGEs have been linked to a variety of serious health concerns, including diabetes, kidney disease, and Alzheimer's.

Make your slow cooker part of your weekly routine. It's an easy step in the right direction toward feeding your family tasty, healthy meals.

SLOW COOKER BASICS

If you've never cooked using a slow cooker before or haven't used one in a while, it's a good idea to start with easier recipes that require few ingredients and shorter cooking times until you become comfortable with your slow cooker. As you gain confidence, move on to entrée recipes that you can prepare in the slow cooker in the morning and let simmer all day. Here are some guidelines for preparing healthy, delicious meals your whole family will love.

Purchase the best-quality ingredients you can find.
Buying good-quality ingredients doesn't mean splurging on artisanal sea salt and pricey cuts of meat. It means choosing fresh produce that's grown locally and is in season (see facing page). The simplest way to gauge freshness is to smell it in the grocery store.

When to Buy In-Season Fruits and Vegetables

Cooking with fresh, local ingredients not only tastes delicious, but it can also reduce your grocery bill. The following is a list of foods that are well suited to slow cooking and when to keep an eye out for them at your local grocer or farmers' market.

SPRING (MARCH TO MAY)

Apricots	Green beans
Artichokes	Peas
Asparagus	Radicchio
Broccoli	Rhubarb
Chives	Snow peas
Collard greens	Sorrel
Fava beans	Swiss chard
Fennel	Watercress

FALL (SEPTEMBER TO NOVEMBER)

Acorn squash	Pears
Belgian endive	Persimmons
Broccoli	Pumpkin
Cabbage	Radicchio
Cauliflower	Rutabagas
Cranberries	Sweet potatoes
Garlic	Swiss chard
Mushrooms	

SUMMER (JUNE TO AUGUST)

Apricots	Jalapeño peppers
Beets	Lima beans
Bell peppers	Peaches
Blackberries	Peas
Blueberries	Plums
Corn	Shallots
Eggplant	Tomatillos
Figs	Tomatoes
French beans	Zucchini
Garlic	

WINTER (DECEMBER TO FEBRUARY)

Brussels sprouts	Squash (various varieties)
Kale	Tangerines
Leeks	Turnips
Oranges	
Parsnips	

Ripe fruit, such as strawberries and cantaloupe, should be sweetly fragrant. Fish and shellfish should never smell fishy; rather, it should smell faintly of the ocean. Meat should look moist and have a pleasing color. Whenever possible, choose organic, free-range, or wild-caught ingredients. Their nutritional profile might be higher than conventionally raised foods, and that comes through in the flavor of the finished product. A study published in the *Journal of Alternative and Complementary Medicine* found that organically grown crops contained "significantly more vitamin C, iron, magnesium, and phosphorus and significantly less nitrates than conventional crops."

Avoid processed, packaged foods.
You don't need to use prepared sauces or salad dressings, which can contain high levels of sodium, preservatives, and other additives your body doesn't need. Cooking with fresh, well-seasoned foods will produce delicious—and much healthier—results.

Cut the fat.
If you're trying to cut calories, you may wish to use a large soup spoon to skim fat from the surface of a finished dish. Alternately, choose very lean cuts of meat and avoid adding additional oil to a recipe.

Hold the salt.
A small amount of salt added at the beginning of the cooking process can help foods release their liquids, but do not season until the food is cooked through. During cooking, the ingredients and cooking liquids will reduce and the flavors will become concentrated. What might seem like the perfect amount of salt initially could taste overly salty after cooking.

Defrost frozen vegetables before adding to the slow cooker.
Defrost frozen vegetables by rinsing them in tepid water for a few minutes before adding them to the slow cooker. This is especially important when they're being cooked with raw meat or dairy products because the slow cooker takes longer to heat frozen items to food-safe temperatures. Nevertheless, frozen vegetables offer a convenient and healthful option for busy families: They're picked at the peak of ripeness, blanched, and then frozen immediately to seal in all their vitamins, minerals, and antioxidants. They're a healthier choice over canned vegetables, which contain additives and sodium and are usually packaged in BPA-lined cans.

When to Choose Organic

The Environmental Working Group (EWG), a nonprofit advocacy organization, compiles an annual list (referred to as "The Dirty Dozen") of the foods most likely to contain residual pesticides, herbicides, and other chemicals used in conventional agriculture practices. As of 2014, the EWG found apples, strawberries, grapes, celery, peaches, spinach, sweet peppers, imported nectarines, cucumbers, cherry tomatoes, imported snap peas, and potatoes to contain the most residual chemicals. In fact, a single sample of nonorganic grapes contained as many as 15 different pesticides, and potatoes contained the most pesticides by weight of any of the fresh fruits and vegetables.

It's not all bad news, though! The EWG also ranks conventionally grown foods that do not contain these levels of pesticides (referred to as the "Clean Fifteen"): avocados, sweet corn, pineapples, cabbage, frozen sweet peas, onions, asparagus, mangos, papayas, kiwis, eggplant, grapefruit, cantaloupe, cauliflower, and sweet potatoes.

Ultimately, the toxins found in processed foods are far worse than the trace amounts of pesticides found in conventional produce, even those on the Dirty Dozen list. Compare a nonorganic fresh strawberry to a candy bar, which is filled with high-fructose corn syrup, artificial colors and flavors, and a host of preservatives. Clearly, the strawberry is a better choice! So when it comes to fresh produce, enjoy as much of it as you can and never let the fear of buying something that's not organic stop you from eating plants. They're good for you!

Save the seafood for the last 30 minutes of cooking.
While most of the recipes in this book do not involve adding any ingredients after the initial preparation, some of the more delicate seafoods, like mussels and scallops, are an exception. They end up overcooked and rubbery if they're cooked for the extended periods of time most other slow cooker recipes call for.

Don't be afraid to use some butter, cream, or sugar—just be sure to follow the instructions and serving sizes recommended in each recipe.
Fat has been vilified over the past several decades, but it is now beginning to be exonerated for the ill effects it was thought to cause. When adding cream or milk to a recipe, aim to add it when the dish is between 140° and 160°F. If the temperature is too high, it will curdle.

Add fresh herbs at the very end of the cooking process.
Leafy herbs such as basil, cilantro, tarragon, and mint taste best when they're added at the very end of the cooking process, as long cooking tends to diminish their flavor. However, dried herbs and those that have woody stems, such as thyme and rosemary, can withstand longer cooking times, and their flavors may even improve with cooking.

▪ ▪ ▪

If you find a recipe in this book that contains an ingredient you don't have on hand or don't like, substitute another ingredient that you do have on hand and enjoy. If your kids aren't crazy about spicy foods, skip the cayenne pepper and allow each person to season his or her own dish. If eggplant is out of season, swap in zucchini or another squash. Discover what works for you, and make each recipe your own.

SHOPPING AND STORAGE TIPS

For most people, daily shopping trips are not only unfeasible, but also they're down-right undesirable. So, how do you shop once a week and keep food fresh until you're ready to use it? Here are a few simple tips and techniques that can keep your grocery budget down and your meals tasting fresh.

Buy in Bulk
Grains, nuts, dried fruit, sugar, and flour are often cheaper when purchased in bulk. Look for them in the bulk section at your local grocer or at dedicated bulk food stores. Keep them fresh by storing them in airtight containers.

Store Wisely
While potatoes and onions make delightful companions in soups and stews, they don't behave nicely when stored together: the compounds they release accelerate deterioration. Store them separately. Apples, particularly bruised apples, also release compounds that can accelerate ripening and even rotting in other fruits and vegetables. Store apples in your refrigerator in a crisper dedicated to fresh produce.

Keep Herbs Fresh
When you purchase fresh herbs, such as cilantro and parsley, treat them as you would fresh flowers. Put them in a small vessel with water (like a vase), and keep them cool, preferably in your refrigerator. Although you wouldn't do this with flowers, cover the

herbs loosely with a plastic bag. For herbs you cannot use in a timely fashion, wash, dry, and store in a resealable bag in the freezer. They will lose their delicate texture, but the flavor will remain intact.

Keep Fish Frozen

At most supermarkets, "fresh" fish has often been previously frozen (usually flash frozen on a fishing vessel for transport) and has been defrosting at the seafood counter for a day or more. Instead, purchase frozen fish and defrost just before you're ready to cook and serve it.

Go Nuts

You already know that fresh fruits and vegetables grow according to season, but did you know that nuts and seeds are best in season as well? Nuts are typically harvested in the fall. Seeds typically follow the harvest season of the plants they come from. To retain freshness, store nuts and seeds in airtight containers (preferably jars) in cool, dark, dry places. (They can quickly go rancid otherwise.)

Store Leftovers Wisely

Follow the same guidelines for storing food that has been cooked in a slow cooker as you would for storing any other cooked foods.

- Place food in a separate container, not the slow cooker's crock. The crock retains heat and will slow cooling. Also, if you plan to reheat the food in the slow cooker, the rapid change in temperature could crack or otherwise damage the crock.

- Choose glass containers for storage to avoid potential toxins released from plastic, particularly if the food is still hot when you transfer it for storage.

- Ensure that the food cools completely in the refrigerator before covering. If you cover it before that time, it will slow the time that the food passes through the "danger zone" between 140F and 40F.

- Leftover meat dishes can be frozen, but vegetable and starch recipes tend to become mushy when frozen and reheated. Fish is equally unsuitable for freezing because it will overcook during the reheating process.

- Store leftovers in the refrigerator for one to three days, the same amount of time you would allow for other cooked foods.

Breakfast and Brunch

■ ■ ■ ■ ■ ■ ■ ■ ■ ■ ■ ■ ■ ■ ■ ■ ■ ■ ■

Homemade Yogurt

GLUTEN-FREE **VEGETARIAN**

MAKES 2 QUARTS, 16 SERVINGS

PREP TIME: 5 MINUTES • COOK TIME: 10½ HOURS

Yogurt is one of the simplest recipes you can create in your slow cooker, and it is also one of the healthiest. Plain yogurt, which eschews the sugar and preservatives often cluttering flavored varieties, is rich in protein and probiotics. Stir in some fresh berries and top with almonds or granola for a delicious breakfast parfait.

8 cups whole milk   ½ cup plain cultured yogurt

1. Pour the milk into the slow cooker.

2. Cover and cook on Low for 2½ hours, until it registers 180°F on a cooking thermometer.

3. Turn off the heat and let the hot milk rest for 2 hours, or until it registers 120°F on a cooking thermometer.

4. Using a clean liquid measuring cup, transfer 1 cup of the warm milk to a small mixing bowl. Add the store-bought yogurt to the bowl and stir thoroughly to combine. Pour the milk-yogurt mixture into the slow cooker. Cover with a thick towel or blanket for 8 hours, to help insulate the mixture.

5. Transfer the yogurt to an airtight container and refrigerate until ready to serve.

Tip: If you want to thicken up your yogurt for a more Greek-style consistency, line a colander with several layers of cheesecloth. Transfer the yogurt to the colander and allow it to drain until you achieve the desired consistency. If you're looking for a very thick yogurt, set the colander over a bowl and refrigerate until it has thickened sufficiently.

Nutritional Information per Serving: Calories: 79; Fat: 4g; Protein: 4g; Carbohydrates: 6g; Sugar: 7g; Sodium: 54mg

Apple Cinnamon Steel-Cut Oatmeal

VEGETARIAN

SERVES 4

PREP TIME: 5 MINUTES • COOK TIME: 8 HOURS ON LOW

Replace your instant oatmeal, which is often processed and high in sugar, with this no-fuss version made with steel-cut oats. Steel-cut oats are dense and chewy (due to the way they are cut) and are an excellent source of protein, soluble and insoluble fiber, and select vitamins and minerals. Prepare everything the night before, and you'll have a healthy, hearty breakfast ready the moment you wake up.

1 tablespoon butter

4 cups water

1 cup steel-cut oats

½ cup walnuts, roughly chopped

2 apples, cored and diced (optional)

1 teaspoon pure vanilla extract (optional)

½ teaspoon ground cinnamon (optional)

1 cup milk, for serving

½ cup raisins, for serving

1. Butter the inside of the slow cooker crock.

2. In the slow cooker, stir together the water, oats, and walnuts, and the apples, vanilla, and cinnamon (if using).

3. Cover and cook on Low for 8 hours.

4. Spoon the oatmeal into serving dishes and top with milk and raisins.

Tip: When purchasing raisins, opt for organic if you can. Grapes make the EWG's Dirty Dozen list year after year for containing high levels of residual pesticides. Choosing organic in this case also helps you avoid the sulfites used in conventional processing.

Nutritional Information per Serving: Calories: 415; Fat: 16g; Protein: 12g; Carbohydrates: 59g; Sugar: 23g; Sodium: 52mg

Orange Cranberry Oatmeal

VEGAN

SERVES 4

PREP TIME: 5 MINUTES • COOK TIME: 8 HOURS ON LOW

Oatmeal provides the complex carbohydrates and fiber to keep you feeling full and energized until lunchtime. The flavors of cranberries, oranges, and cloves make this the perfect wintertime breakfast.

3 cups water

1 cup old-fashioned rolled oats

½ cup dried unsweetened cranberries

Zest and juice of 1 orange

⅛ teaspoon ground cloves

Pinch sea salt

1. In the slow cooker, stir together the water, oats, cranberries, orange zest and juice, cloves, and salt.

2. Cover and cook on Low for 8 hours.

   Tip: Unsweetened dried cranberries keep the sugar content of this breakfast in check. If you cannot find them, consider using 1 cup fresh cranberries.

   Nutritional Information per Serving: Calories: 139; Fat: 2g; Protein: 4g; Carbohydrates: 27g; Sugar: 9g; Sodium: 59mg

Hearty Quinoa
with Cherries and Almonds

GLUTEN-FREE **VEGETARIAN**

SERVES 4

PREP TIME: 5 MINUTES • COOK TIME: 2 HOURS ON HIGH OR 8 HOURS ON LOW

Quinoa is equally at home in sweet and savory recipes. This breakfast dish combines the ancient grain with dried cherries and almonds for a meal that's rich in antioxidants, protein, and healthy fats.

1 cup quinoa, rinsed and drained

3 cups milk

1 cup dried unsweetened cherries

1 cup slivered almonds

Pinch sea salt

1. In the slow cooker, gently mix the quinoa, milk, cherries, almonds, and salt.

2. Cover and cook on High for 2 hours or on Low for 8 hours.

Nutritional Highlight: Quinoa is one of the richest sources of plant-based protein and is naturally gluten-free.

Nutritional Information per Serving: Calories: 466; Fat: 18g; Protein: 19g; Carbohydrates: 66g; Sugar: 28g; Sodium: 157mg

Coconut Quinoa Porridge

GLUTEN-FREE **VEGAN**

SERVES 4

PREP TIME: 5 MINUTES • COOK TIME: 2 HOURS ON HIGH OR 8 HOURS ON LOW

Quinoa and coconut milk provide a rich, filling breakfast treat. Quinoa is an excellent source of protein and contains complex carbohydrates, which make you feel full longer. Coconut milk contains healthy fats, which your body needs for energy and building healthy cells. For an extra special treat, toast unsweetened shredded coconut briefly under the broiler and sprinkle on your porridge just before serving.

3 cups coconut milk

1 cup quinoa, rinsed and drained

1 teaspoon pure vanilla extract

Pinch sea salt

¼ cup unsweetened shredded coconut, toasted, for serving (optional)

1. In the slow cooker, mix the coconut milk, quinoa, vanilla, and salt.

2. Cover and cook on High for 2 hours or on Low for 8 hours.

3. Serve with toasted coconut (if using).

Nutritional Highlight: Coconut milk is heart healthy and can help increase nutrient absorption and stimulate metabolism.

Nutritional Information per Serving: Calories: 374; Fat: 24g; Protein: 8g; Carbohydrates: 34g; Sugar: 3g; Sodium: 82mg

Maple Vanilla "Oven" Pancake

VEGETARIAN

SERVES 4

PREP TIME: 5 MINUTES • COOK TIME: 1 HOUR ON HIGH

An oven pancake is traditionally prepared and baked in one dish, freeing the maker from all the pouring and flipping necessary for stove-top pancakes. Turn off the oven and make this simple and delicious pancake in your slow cooker. Kids will love its subtle sweetness while you enjoy that it's homemade and free of all the additives in most commercially prepared mixes.

1 tablespoon butter

1 cup all-purpose flour

½ cup milk

¼ cup pure maple syrup

2 teaspoons pure vanilla extract

5 eggs

1. Butter the inside of the slow cooker crock.

2. In a bowl, mix the flour, milk, maple syrup, vanilla, and eggs, and stir until smooth. Pour the egg mixture into the slow cooker.

3. Cover and cook on High for 1 hour, or until the pancake is cooked through and a toothpick inserted in the center comes out clean.

Tip: For the most intense maple flavor, choose Grade B maple syrup. It might sound substandard to Grade A, but it is harvested well into the season and is the darkest, richest option.

Nutritional Information per Serving: Calories: 291; Fat: 9g; Protein: 11g; Carbohydrates: 39g; Sugar: 14g; Sodium: 114mg

Breakfast Quiche

GLUTEN-FREE **VEGETARIAN**

SERVES 4

PREP TIME: 20 MINUTES • COOK TIME: 8 HOURS ON LOW

You can customize this simple, crustless breakfast quiche to your taste or simply enjoy it as is. Think of it as a cheese omelet for the whole family—but with no flipping or dirtying of multiple pans. Bonus: It's loaded with protein and healthy fats to keep your family feeling full for hours.

1 tablespoon butter	Sea salt
6 eggs	Freshly ground black pepper
½ cup milk	1 cup shredded sharp Cheddar cheese

1. Butter the inside of the slow cooker crock.

2. Whisk together the eggs and milk and season with salt and pepper. Stir in the cheese. Pour mixture into the slow cooker.

3. Cover and cook on Low for 8 hours.

Nutritional Highlight: If you're concerned about saturated fat intake, know that an even greater percentage of fat in egg yolks is monounsaturated fat, which has been shown to reduce the risk of heart disease.

Nutritional Information per Serving: Calories: 249; Fat: 19g; Protein: 16g; Carbohydrates: 2g; Sugar: 2g; Sodium: 361mg

Fennel Sausage Breakfast Casserole

SERVES 4

PREP TIME: 20 MINUTES • COOK TIME: 8 HOURS ON LOW

When you want a decadent brunch dish, turn to this one-dish wonder—the Italian sausage and fontina cheese give it loads of flavor.

1 tablespoon butter

8 ounces fennel sausage,
   casings removed

¼ cup diced red onion

¼ cup minced fresh basil leaves

1 cup shredded fontina cheese

6 eggs

½ cup milk

Sea salt

Freshly ground black pepper

1. Butter the inside of the slow cooker crock.

2. In a medium skillet over medium heat, sauté the sausage until browned and just cooked through. Set aside.

3. In the slow cooker, mix the cooked sausage, onion, basil, and cheese.

4. In a small bowl, whisk together the eggs and milk and season with salt and pepper. Pour over the sausage mixture and stir gently to combine. Cook on Low for 8 hours.

Tip: If you are concerned about the fat content in this dish, choose lean sausages (or omit them entirely for a meatless version) and replace the fontina cheese with your favorite low-fat cheese. It won't be as decadent, but it will still taste great.

Nutritional Information per Serving: Calories: 437; Fat: 33g; Protein: 28g; Carbohydrates: 5g; Sugar: 4g; Sodium: 915mg

Cinnamon Swirl Coffee Cake

VEGETARIAN

SERVES 4 TO 6

PREP TIME: 15 MINUTES • COOK TIME: 3 HOURS ON HIGH

This classic coffee cake recipe is made a little healthier with whole-grain flour for more fiber and nutrients. Whole wheat pastry flour has been processed to remain light and fluffy in baked goods, so you won't notice the difference between this and a less healthy version of your favorite breakfast pastry.

FOR THE STREUSEL TOPPING

¼ cup whole wheat pastry flour

¼ cup old-fashioned rolled oats

3 tablespoons butter, at room
   temperature

1 tablespoon brown sugar

½ teaspoon ground cinnamon

FOR THE CAKE

½ cup butter, melted, divided

1½ cups whole wheat pastry flour

1 teaspoon baking soda

¼ teaspoon salt

½ cup brown sugar

2 eggs

½ cup milk, divided

1 tablespoon ground cinnamon

To make the topping

Mix the flour, oats, butter, sugar, and cinnamon in a food processor fitted with the metal blade, and pulse until the mixture resembles coarse sand. Set aside.

To make the cake

1. Butter the inside of your slow cooker with one tablespoon of melted butter.

2. In a large bowl, sift together the flour, baking soda, and salt.

3. In a small bowl, using an electric mixer, mix the sugar, the remaining 7 table-spoons of melted butter, the eggs, and ¼ cup milk until smooth. Pour the wet ingredients into the dry ingredients and stir until just combined. Pour the cake batter into the crock of the slow cooker.

4. In a small liquid measuring cup, whisk together the cinnamon and the remaining ¼ cup milk. Pour over the cake batter, then use a toothpick or knife to draw swirls into the cinnamon mixture. Do not stir—allow the swirls to remain.

5. Sprinkle the top of the batter with the prepared streusel topping.

6. Cover and cook on High for 2½ hours. Remove the lid and continue cooking for another 30 minutes, until browned around the edges and set in the middle.

Nutritional Highlight: In a study published in the *American Journal of Clinical Nutrition*, the addition of about ¼ teaspoon of cinnamon in a serving of dessert was shown to reduce the after-meal blood glucose response—so when you enjoy a slice of this coffee cake, your insulin levels are less likely to rise and fall dramatically. Delicious flavor and sustained energy sound like a pretty good combination!

Nutritional Information per Serving: Calories: 625; Fat: 36g; Protein: 10g; Carbohydrates: 66g; Sugar: 22g; Sodium: 738mg

Soups and Stews

Sweet Potato Bisque

GLUTEN-FREE **VEGETARIAN**

SERVES 6

PREP TIME: 5 MINUTES • COOK TIME: 6 TO 8 HOURS ON LOW

Sweet potatoes are, not surprisingly, naturally sweet. So, unless you're making dessert, you may want to balance them with savory flavors. In this hearty bisque, leeks and herbs complement the root vegetable.

4 cups vegetable broth

6 cups diced sweet potatoes

2 leeks, white and pale green
parts only, diced

2 fresh thyme sprigs

Sea salt

Freshly ground black pepper

½ cup heavy or whipping (35%) cream

1. In the slow cooker, mix the broth, sweet potatoes, leeks, and thyme. Season with salt and pepper.

2. Cover and cook on Low for 6 to 8 hours. Discard the thyme sprigs.

3. Using a stand or immersion blender, purée the soup. Stir in the cream. Serve warm.

Variation: To make a vegan version of this soup, substitute coconut cream for the whipping cream.

Nutritional Information per Serving: Calories: 255; Fat: 5g; Protein: 6g; Carbohydrates: 47g; Sugar: 2g; Sodium: 571 mg

Apple and Celeriac Purée

SERVES 4

PREP TIME: 5 MINUTES • COOK TIME: 2 TO 4 HOURS ON LOW

Celeriac, often called celery root, adds creaminess to this soup the same way potatoes do but contains one-third of the carbohydrates. Don't worry if you're not normally a fan of celery—the root has a much more delicate flavor than celery stalks.

1 pound celeriac, peeled and diced

2 tart cooking apples, peeled, cored, and diced

4 cups chicken broth

Sea salt

Freshly ground black pepper

½ cup sour cream, for serving

Fresh chives, for serving

1. In the slow cooker, mix the celeriac, apples, and broth. Season with salt and pepper.

2. Cover and cook on Low for 2 to 4 hours.

3. Using a stand or immersion blender, purée the soup. Serve warm garnished with sour cream and chives.

Nutritional Highlight: Celeriac is ultra-low in calories, with less than 70 calories per cup. It also contains relatively high amounts of protein and fiber and is rich in vitamins C and B_6.

Nutritional Information per Serving: Calories: 195; Fat: 8g; Protein: 8g; Carbohydrates: 25g; Sugar: 12g; Sodium: 951mg

Creamy Carrot Soup

GLUTEN-FREE **VEGETARIAN**

SERVES 4

PREP TIME: 5 MINUTES • COOK TIME: 6 TO 8 HOURS ON LOW

Carrots are an incredible source of vitamin A, supplying more than 200 percent of your daily value in just 1 medium carrot. Complement their natural sweetness with sage and orange for a flavorful, creamy soup.

2 pounds carrots, diced

4 cups vegetable broth

1 fresh sage sprig

Zest and juice of 1 orange

Sea salt

Freshly ground black pepper

½ cup sour cream, for serving

1. In the slow cooker, mix the carrots, broth, sage, and orange zest and juice. Season generously with salt and pepper.

2. Cover and cook on Low for 6 to 8 hours. Discard the sage.

3. Using an immersion blender, purée until smooth.

4. Serve with a dollop of sour cream.

Variation: Adjust the seasonings to suit your mood. Swap the orange juice for lime juice and add a teaspoon of fresh grated ginger for an Asian feel. Or add a pinch each of cinnamon and nutmeg.

Nutritional Information per Serving: Calories: 216; Fat: 8g; Protein: 8g; Carbohydrates: 30g; Sugar: 16g; Sodium: 993mg

Cream of Broccoli Soup

VEGETARIAN

SERVES 4 TO 6

PREP TIME: 10 MINUTES • COOK TIME: 4 HOURS ON LOW

It can be hard to find a slow cooker recipe for cream of broccoli soup that doesn't contain a can of cream of something soup or condensed milk. This recipe uses only fresh, whole ingredients to create a meal you can feel good about.

1 tablespoon butter

1 onion, diced

1 tablespoon all-purpose flour

2 pounds broccoli florets

4 cups chicken or vegetable broth

¼ cup heavy or whipping (35%) cream

1 cup shredded cheese

1. In a large skillet over medium heat, melt the butter. Cook the onion for 5 to 7 minutes, until translucent. Stir in the flour until well combined. Transfer the mixture to the slow cooker. Add the broccoli and broth.

2. Cover and cook on Low until the broccoli is tender, about 4 hours.

3. Turn off the heat and stir in the cream until combined. Stir in the cheese. Serve warm.

Tip: Be careful when adding dairy products to a hot soup. If the temperature is too high, they will curdle. Aim to add dairy when the dish is between 140° and 160°F.

Nutritional Information per Serving: Calories: 300; Fat: 17g; Protein: 19g; Carbohydrates: 21g; Sugar: 6g; Sodium: 1,037mg

Cream of Mushroom Soup

GLUTEN-FREE **VEGETARIAN**

SERVES 6

PREP TIME: 10 MINUTES • COOK TIME: 8 HOURS ON LOW

You'll never go back to the gloppy canned stuff again after trying this rich, flavorful cream of mushroom soup. Not only does it taste better, but it's also better for you—with far less sodium and saturated fat than the store-bought variety.

2 ounces dried mushrooms, soaked in hot water for 10 minutes, then rinsed and finely diced

4 cups sliced fresh mushrooms

4 cups chicken or vegetable broth

¼ cup sherry (optional)

1 tablespoon butter

1 onion, diced

4 garlic cloves, smashed

4 fresh thyme sprigs

Sea salt

Freshly ground black pepper

½ cup heavy or whipping (35%) cream

1. In the slow cooker, mix the mushrooms, broth, sherry (if using), butter, onion, garlic, and thyme. Season with salt and pepper.

2. Cover and cook on Low for 8 hours. Discard the thyme sprigs.

3. Transfer 2 cups of the mixture to a blender and purée until smooth. Pour back into the slow cooker and stir to combine. Stir in cream. Serve warm.

Nutritional Highlight: Mushrooms contain glutamic acid, a natural version of the flavor enhancer MSG, which explains why they taste so rich. Unlike the food additive, mushrooms are good for you. They contain potassium, copper, riboflavin, and pantothenic acid.

Nutritional Information per Serving: Calories: 110; Fat: 7g; Protein: 6g; Carbohydrates: 5g; Sugar: 2g; Sodium: 569mg

Tomato Basil Soup

GLUTEN-FREE **VEGETARIAN** **PALEO-FRIENDLY**

SERVES 4

PREP TIME: 10 MINUTES • COOK TIME: 4 TO 6 HOURS ON LOW

While you can easily make this soup on the stove top, cooking tomato soup in the slow cooker provides a richer, more robust flavor due to the slow, gentle heat. The basil is added at the beginning to flavor the broth and then used again as a garnish for a hint of fresh basil flavor.

2 (28-ounce) cans plum tomatoes, with juice, broken apart and seeded

2 cups chicken or vegetable broth

2 tablespoons olive oil

4 garlic cloves, minced

2 fresh basil sprigs, plus more for serving

Sea salt

Freshly ground black pepper

1. In the slow cooker, mix the tomatoes, broth, oil, garlic, and basil. Season with salt and pepper.

2. Cover and cook on Low for 4 to 6 hours. Discard the basil sprigs.

3. Serve garnished with fresh basil.

Tip: Fresh basil imparts far superior flavor compared to dried basil. It can, however, sometimes be difficult to use up a bunch of fresh basil. Freezing the herb works surprisingly well. Simply rinse and dry the basil leaves thoroughly and store in a resealable freezer bag. Use frozen basil in soups or sauces when texture is less important.

Nutritional Information per Serving: Calories: 262; Fat: 10g; Protein: 25g; Carbohydrates: 21g; Sugar: 16g; Sodium: 155mg

Manhattan Clam Chowder

GLUTEN-FREE

SERVES 4 TO 6

PREP TIME: 10 MINUTES • COOK TIME: 4 TO 6 HOURS ON LOW

New England clam chowder is loaded with fat and calories. This Manhattan version, which has a tomato, rather than cream, base, has dramatically fewer calories and negligible saturated fat.

4 cups fish or chicken broth

2 cups diced yellow potatoes

1 (15-ounce) can plum tomatoes, with juice

1 cup diced onion

1 cup diced celery

½ cup dry white wine

¼ cup minced fresh parsley leaves

2 fresh thyme sprigs

2 garlic cloves, minced

Sea salt

Freshly ground black pepper

2 pounds fresh clams

1. In the slow cooker, mix the broth, potatoes, tomatoes, onion, celery, wine, parsley, thyme, and garlic. Season with salt and pepper.

2. Cover and cook on Low for 4 to 6 hours, or until the potatoes are tender.

3. Add fresh clams to the slow cooker, cover, and continue cooking until nearly all of them have opened. Discard the clamshells and any unopened clams.

Tip: If desired, you can replace the fresh clams with 6 ounces of canned clams, drained, rinsed, and roughly chopped. Stir into the soup just before serving.

Nutritional Information per Serving: Calories: 173; Fat: 2g; Protein: 9g; Carbohydrates: 26g; Sugar: 8g; Sodium: 868mg

THE HEALTHY SLOW COOKER COOKBOOK

Chicken Chowder

GLUTEN-FREE

SERVES 4 TO 6

PREP TIME: 20 MINUTES • COOK TIME: 6 TO 8 HOURS ON LOW

You might think bacon and cream don't belong in a recipe purporting to be healthy, but one piece of bacon has only about 45 calories and only a minimal amount of cream is used here to add flavor. (Use less or skip it entirely if you want a lighter soup.)

1 bacon slice

1 onion, diced

4 garlic cloves, minced

4 cups chicken broth

2 cups cubed cooked chicken

2 cups diced yellow potatoes

2 cups corn kernels (thawed if frozen)

4 fresh thyme sprigs

Sea salt

Freshly ground black pepper

½ cup heavy or whipping (35%) cream

2 scallions, white and green parts, thinly sliced

1. In a large skillet over medium-low heat, cook the bacon for 10 to 15 minutes, until browned and the fat has been rendered. Transfer the cooked bacon to a cutting board, reserving the fat, and chop into pieces.

2. In the same skillet, cook the onion and garlic until softened. Transfer the onion mixture and bacon pieces to the slow cooker. Add the broth, chicken, potatoes, corn, and thyme. Season with salt and pepper.

3. Cover and cook on Low for 6 to 8 hours.

4. Just before serving, stir in the cream and scallions.

Tip: If your scallions seem to go bad before you can use them, make sure you're storing them properly. Wrap them in a moist paper towel, and then wrap in plastic wrap.

Nutritional Information per Serving: Calories: 375; Fat: 11g; Protein: 34g; Carbohydrates: 37g; Sugar: 6g; Sodium: 898mg

Chicken and Zucchini "Noodle" Soup

GLUTEN-FREE **PALEO-FRIENDLY**

SERVES 4 TO 6

PREP TIME: 15 MINUTES • COOK TIME: 4 HOURS ON LOW

The addition of zucchini noodles is a nice, light twist on this comfort-food favorite. If you don't have a spiralizer, use a vegetable peeler or mandoline to make "fettuccine" noodles.

2 cups diced carrots

2 cups diced celery

8 garlic cloves, smashed

1 pound boneless chicken thighs, diced

8 cups chicken broth

2 fresh thyme sprigs

Sea salt

Freshly ground black pepper

2 large zucchini, peeled and cut into "noodles"

1. In the slow cooker, mix the carrots, celery, garlic, chicken, broth, and thyme. Season with salt and pepper.

2. Cover and cook on Low for 4 hours, or until the chicken is cooked through.

3. In the last 20 minutes of cooking, season the zucchini noodles generously with salt and set in a colander to drain for 15 minutes. Rinse and, using your hands, squeeze out the excess moisture. Add the zucchini noodles to the slow cooker and cook until just heated through, about 2 minutes.

Nutritional Highlight: Swapping zucchini for pasta slashes calories by more than 75 percent. And zucchini is rich in magnesium, vitamins C and B_6, and fiber.

Nutritional Information per Serving: Calories: 384; Fat: 20g; Protein: 33g; Carbohydrates: 16g; Sugar: 8g; Sodium: 1,773mg

Thai Sweet and Sour Soup

GLUTEN-FREE VEGETARIAN

SERVES 4

PREP TIME: 5 MINUTES • COOK TIME: 2 TO 4 HOURS ON LOW

This soup is delicious made with chicken or, vegetarian-style, with tofu and vegetable broth. Just don't skip the lime leaves. They give this soup an intoxicating aroma and delicious flavor that permeates the broth during slow cooking.

1 onion, thinly sliced

4 garlic cloves, minced

1 teaspoon minced fresh ginger

4 cups chicken or vegetable broth

2 tablespoons hot and sour paste

4 Kaffir lime leaves

2 tablespoons fish sauce

2 cups diced cooked chicken or tofu

4 ounces rice noodles

Lime wedges, for serving

Fresh cilantro, for serving

1. In the slow cooker, mix the onion, garlic, ginger, broth, hot and sour paste, and lime leaves.

2. Cover and cook on Low for 2 to 4 hours.

3. Stir in the fish sauce, chicken, and rice noodles. Cover and cook for 10 minutes, or until the noodles are softened and the chicken is heated through.

4. Serve with lime wedges and cilantro.

Tip: You can find Kaffir lime leaves at most Asian markets. Store any that you don't use in an airtight container in the freezer, where they will keep for several months.

Nutritional Information per Serving: Calories: 203; Fat: 7g; Protein: 17g; Carbohydrates: 19g; Sugar: 4g; Sodium: 1,857mg

Turkey and Wild Rice Soup

SERVES 4 TO 6

PREP TIME: 10 MINUTES • COOK TIME: 4 TO 6 HOURS ON LOW

This is a simple and delicious way to use up leftover holiday turkey. If you're feeling particularly ambitious, make your own turkey broth. (See the following Tip.)

4 cups chicken broth or homemade
    turkey broth

4 cups cooked turkey, cut into
    bite-size pieces

1 cup wild rice

1 onion, diced

2 garlic cloves, minced

2 carrots, diced

2 celery stalks, diced

1 teaspoon dried Italian herb blend

Sea salt

Freshly ground black pepper

1. In the slow cooker, mix the broth, turkey, rice, onion, garlic, carrots, celery, and herbs. Season with salt and pepper.

2. Cover and cook on Low for 4 to 6 hours, or until the rice is cooked.

Tip: To make your own turkey broth, put the turkey carcass in the slow cooker. Cover with 12 cups of cold water. Add an onion, one or two stalks of celery, and a large carrot, chopped, season with salt and pepper, and cook on Low for 8 hours. Let the broth cool, then strain. (Discard cooking solids.)

Nutritional Information per Serving: Calories: 448; Fat: 9g; Protein: 52g; Carbohydrates: 37g; Sugar: 5g; Sodium: 892mg

Italian Wedding Soup

SERVES 4

PREP TIME: 5 MINUTES • COOK TIME: 2 HOURS ON LOW

In Italian, this soup is called minestra maritata, *which means "married soup," a reference to the flavorful marriage of greens and meat. Whatever you call it, the pairing is a match made in heaven. Just go easy on the salt. The chicken sausage will infuse the broth with flavor that intensifies through cooking.*

4 cups chicken broth

16 ounces precooked chicken sausage, cut into 1-inch chunks

1 cup orzo pasta

1 large bunch Tuscan ("dinosaur") kale, center rib removed and thinly sliced

1 onion, diced

1 teaspoon dried Italian herb blend

Pinch red pepper flakes

Sea salt

Freshly ground black pepper

1. In the slow cooker, mix the broth, sausage, orzo, kale, onion, herbs, and red pepper flakes. Season lightly with salt and pepper.

2. Cover and cook on Low for 2 hours, until orzo is tender.

Tip: To prepare the kale, cut out the thick center rib. Stack the leaves on top of one another, roll lengthwise into a tight cylinder, and, using a sharp knife, cut crosswise into thin slices. (This technique is called a chiffonade.)

Nutritional Highlight: Precooked chicken sausage contains far fewer calories and less fat than similar sausages made with pork. Try making this dish with a sweet or spicy Italian-style sausage.

Nutritional Information per Serving: Calories: 198; Fat: 5g; Protein: 15g; Carbohydrates: 23g; Sugar: 2g; Sodium: 1,034mg

Lentil Soup with Sausage

GLUTEN-FREE

SERVES 4

PREP TIME: 10 MINUTES • COOK TIME: 8 HOURS ON LOW

Just a little sausage goes a long way in this flavorful, fiber-rich soup.

1 tablespoon olive oil

1 hot sausage link, crumbled

1 cup diced carrots

1 cup diced celery

1 onion, diced

2 garlic cloves, minced

4 cups chicken broth

½ cup white wine

1½ cups green lentils

Sea salt

Freshly ground black pepper

1. In a large skillet over medium heat, brown the sausage in the oil for 1 to 2 minutes. Add the carrots, celery, onion, and garlic, and cook for about 5 minutes, until the vegetables are softened.

2. Transfer the mixture to the slow cooker. Add the chicken broth, wine, and lentils. Season with salt and pepper.

3. Cover and cook on Low for 8 hours.

Variation: For a vegetarian soup, swap the chicken broth for vegetable broth and the sausage for 1 cup of mushrooms and 1 cup of shredded kale or other dark leafy green.

Nutritional Information per Serving: Calories: 388; Fat: 7g; Protein: 25g; Carbohydrates: 52g; Sugar: 6g; Sodium: 895mg

Beef Pho

GLUTEN-FREE

SERVES 4

PREP TIME: 10 MINUTES • COOK TIME: 6 TO 8 HOURS ON LOW

This Vietnamese soup has become a hipster favorite, with posh pho restaurants popping up all over the country. Skip the scene and make it at home with a few authentic ingredients. Although rice noodles are a quintessential ingredient in pho, if you're following a low-carb diet, you can substitute bean sprouts or zucchini noodles or simply skip the noodles altogether.

1 pound beef sirloin, thinly sliced

1 large onion, thinly sliced

1 teaspoon minced fresh ginger

1 teaspoon ground coriander

1 teaspoon ground cloves

¼ teaspoon ground cinnamon

1 tablespoon fennel seeds

4 cups vegetable or beef broth

2 tablespoons fish sauce

4 ounces Vietnamese rice noodles

Chopped fresh cilantro, for serving

1. In the slow cooker, mix the beef, onion, and spices. Pour in the broth.

2. Cover and cook on Low for 6 to 8 hours.

3. About 10 minutes before serving, pour in the fish sauce and stir in the rice noodles. Set aside, covered, until the noodles are soft.

4. Serve with fresh cilantro.

Variation: If you prefer, substitute an equal amount of soy sauce for the fish sauce.

Nutritional Information per Serving: Calories: 308; Fat: 9g; Protein: 41g; Carbohydrates: 13g; Sugar: 3g; Sodium: 1,541mg

Appetizers and Sides

Cheese Fondue

VEGETARIAN

SERVES 8

PREP TIME: 5 MINUTES • COOK TIME: 1 TO 2 HOURS ON LOW

Fondue is tricky. It can conceal all manner of sins—namely an excess of saturated fat and sodium—without much flavor, or it can be decadent and rich in flavor without those pesky extra calories. The best fondue recipes use Swiss cheese, which has a greater ratio of protein to fat than other medium-hard cheeses. In fact, just 1 ounce of Swiss cheese contains 8 grams of protein. Instead of the traditional cubed bread for dipping, go low carb with raw carrots, broccoli, and cauliflower.

8 ounces Swiss cheese, shredded

8 ounces sharp Cheddar cheese, shredded

1 garlic clove, minced

½ teaspoon dry mustard

¼ teaspoon freshly grated nutmeg

2 tablespoons all-purpose flour

1 cup light beer

1. In the slow cooker, mix the cheeses, garlic, dry mustard, nutmeg, and flour. Pour in the beer.

2. Cover and cook on Low for 1 to 2 hours, or until the cheese is melted.

3. Uncover and stir well. Serve the fondue from the slow cooker, keeping the heat on Low.

Tip: For a nonalcoholic version, simply substitute 1 cup of milk for the beer.

Nutritional Information per Serving: Calories: 240; Fat: 17g; Protein: 13g; Carbohydrates: 4g; Sugar: 1g; Sodium: 232mg

French Onion Dip

GLUTEN-FREE **VEGETARIAN**

SERVES 12

PREP TIME: 5 MINUTES • COOK TIME: 6 TO 8 HOURS ON HIGH

Skip the packaged French onion dressing and make your own French onion dip. Unlike caramelizing onions on the stove top, doing it in a slow cooker means you needn't stand over the pot stirring constantly. This recipe works best when left to cook overnight.

4 onions, thinly sliced

2 tablespoons olive oil

1 tablespoon butter

Sea salt

Pinch granulated sugar

½ cup sour cream

½ cup mayonnaise

Freshly ground black pepper

1. In the slow cooker, mix the onions, oil, and butter. Season with salt and sugar.

2. Cover and cook on High for 6 to 8 hours, or until the onions are a rich, dark brown.

3. Transfer the cooked onions to a food processor fitted with the metal blade. Process until still slightly chunky. Add the sour cream and mayonnaise and pulse until thoroughly combined. Season with salt and pepper.

Tip: If you want to avoid the additives in store-bought mayonnaise, you can easily make your own. Simply whisk together 1 teaspoon lemon juice, 1 teaspoon water, and 1 egg yolk in a warm bowl. Slowly whisk in olive oil, one drop at a time, until the sauce thickens, adding up to ½ cup of oil.

Nutritional Information per Serving: Calories: 103; Fat: 9g; Protein: 1g; Carbohydrates: 6g; Sugar: 2g; Sodium: 101mg

Navy Bean Dip

GLUTEN-FREE **VEGAN**

MAKES 4 CUPS, 8 SERVINGS

PREP TIME: 5 MINUTES • COOK TIME: 1 TO 2 HOURS ON LOW

Navy beans earned their name when they became a wartime staple in the early 1900s. They're creamy in texture and loaded with protein, making them a perfect base for a healthy dip. Serve the dip directly from the slow cooker to keep it warm.

1 tablespoon mashed roasted garlic
   (see the following Tip)

2 (15-ounce) cans navy beans, rinsed
   and drained

¼ teaspoon sea salt

1 teaspoon fresh thyme leaves

Zest and juice of 1 lemon

2 tablespoons olive oil

1. In the slow cooker, mix the garlic, beans, salt, thyme, lemon zest and juice, and oil.

2. Cover and cook on Low for 1 to 2 hours, or until heated through and the flavors have melded.

3. Using a potato masher or the back of a fork, mash the mixture until you achieve the desired consistency. Serve warm.

Tip: To roast garlic, preheat the oven to 375°F. Cut off and discard the top of a head of garlic. Put the bulb in the center of a square of aluminum foil. Drizzle with 1 teaspoon olive oil. Wrap the foil loosely around the garlic and roast for about 45 minutes. Unwrap and cool completely. Squeeze each of the garlic cloves from its skin.

Nutritional Information per Serving: Calories: 164; Fat: 4g; Protein: 9g; Carbohydrates: 25g; Sugar: 0g; Sodium: 561mg

THE HEALTHY SLOW COOKER COOKBOOK

Edamame Miso Dip

GLUTEN-FREE **VEGAN**

MAKES 4 CUPS, 8 SERVINGS

PREP TIME: 5 MINUTES • COOK TIME: 1 TO 2 HOURS ON LOW

Edamame are fresh young soybeans. Preparing them in a slow cooker allows ample time for the miso to infuse them with flavor.

1 (16-ounce) bag frozen, shelled edamame	Juice of 1 lime
2 cups vegetable broth or water	Sea salt
2 tablespoons white miso	Freshly ground black pepper

1. In the slow cooker, mix the edamame, broth, and miso.

2. Cover and cook on Low for 1 to 2 hours. Using a potato masher or the back of a fork, mash the mixture until you achieve the desired consistency. Stir in the lime juice and season with salt and pepper.

3. Serve warm or chilled.

Tip: If you cannot find shelled edamame, you can substitute two 16-ounce bags of edamame still in their pods. Thaw before shelling.

Nutritional Information per Serving: Calories: 94; Fat: 2g; Protein: 9g; Carbohydrates: 10g; Sugar: 2g; Sodium: 392mg

Shrimp and Artichoke Dip

SERVES 24

PREP TIME: 10 MINUTES • COOK TIME: 2 HOURS ON LOW

Serve this savory dip with celery and carrots for a pleasing contrast of flavor and texture. Because this dish is very rich, a little goes a long way, so opt for just a ¼ cup serving. Nevertheless, it's rich in protein and even sneaks in a few vegetables.

8 ounces cooked, peeled, deveined
    shrimp, diced

1 (14-ounce) jar artichoke hearts,
    drained and roughly chopped

¼ cup sliced scallions

1 cup sour cream

1 cup milk

¼ cup freshly grated Parmesan cheese

2 garlic cloves, crushed

⅓ cup mayonnaise

1 tablespoon red wine vinegar

8 ounces cream cheese, cubed

Sea salt

Freshly ground black pepper

1. In the slow cooker, mix the shrimp, artichoke hearts, scallions, sour cream, milk, Parmesan, garlic, mayonnaise, and vinegar. Put the cream cheese on top.

2. Cover and cook on Low for 2 hours. Stir well and season with salt and pepper.

Nutritional Information per Serving: Calories: 93; Fat: 7g; Protein: 4g; Carbohydrates: 4g; Sugar: 1g; Sodium: 102mg

Sweet Potato Pudding

GLUTEN-FREE   **VEGETARIAN**   **PALEO-FRIENDLY**

SERVES 6 TO 8

PREP TIME: 5 MINUTES • COOK TIME: 4 TO 6 HOURS ON LOW

The natural sweetness of sweet potatoes intensifies with cooking, making marshmallows and brown sugar unnecessary additions. Instead, swap the sticky holiday dish for this fluffy sweet potato pudding. It contains far fewer calories and less than half of the sugar of the original version.

2 pounds sweet potatoes,
   peeled and diced

1 shallot, minced

4 cups unfiltered apple cider

Sea salt

Freshly ground black pepper

2 tablespoons butter

1. In the slow cooker, mix the sweet potatoes, shallot, and apple cider. Season generously with salt and pepper.

2. Cover and cook on Low for 4 to 6 hours, or until the sweet potatoes are tender.

3. Using an immersion blender or a potato masher, purée the mixture. Stir in the butter.

Nutritional Highlight: Sweet potatoes are rich in fiber and contain vitamin B_6 and iron. They also have a lower glycemic index than potatoes, making them a healthier choice.

Nutritional Information per Serving: Calories: 291; Fat: 4g; Protein: 3g; Carbohydrates: 62g; Sugar: 19g; Sodium: 85mg

Jalapeño Corn Pudding

GLUTEN-FREE **VEGETARIAN**

SERVES 6 TO 8

PREP TIME: 10 MINUTES • COOK TIME: 2 TO 3 HOURS ON LOW

This recipe requires a bit of preparation before it's put into the slow cooker, but the results are delicious. It's perfect for when you don't feel like heating up the kitchen but want a savory side dish.

4 cups milk

½ cup polenta or yellow cornmeal

4 to 6 ears fresh corn, kernels removed

¼ cup thinly sliced scallions

2 garlic cloves, minced

1 teaspoon fresh thyme

1 jalapeño pepper, seeded for a milder heat, minced

Sea salt

Freshly ground black pepper

3 eggs, yolks and whites separated

1 tablespoon butter

1. In a saucepan over medium heat, bring the milk to a gentle simmer. Slowly whisk in the cornmeal. Add the corn, scallions, garlic, thyme, and jalapeño, and stir to combine. Season with salt and pepper. One at a time, stir in the egg yolks.

2. In a separate bowl, whisk the egg whites until stiff peaks form. Fold into the corn mixture.

3. Butter the inside of the slow cooker crock. Gently transfer the corn pudding batter to the slow cooker.

4. Cover and cook on Low for 2 to 3 hours, or until the center is set.

Tip: This recipe works equally well using 2 cups of frozen corn.

Nutritional Information per Serving: Calories: 219; Fat: 8g; Protein: 11g; Carbohydrates: 29g; Sugar: 9g; Sodium: 162mg

Warm Olives with Herbs and Almonds

GLUTEN-FREE **VEGAN** **PALEO-FRIENDLY**

SERVES 8

PREP TIME: 5 MINUTES • COOK TIME: 6 HOURS ON LOW

When you're preparing for a party, the last thing you want to do is stand over a hot stove or heat up your kitchen with the oven. Use your slow cooker to prepare this healthy appetizer while you prepare other dishes. Olives and almonds are infused with the rustic flavors of rosemary and thyme.

1 cup almonds

2 cups mixed olives

1 fresh rosemary sprig

1 fresh thyme sprig

¼ cup olive oil

Sea salt

Freshly ground black pepper

¼ cup sherry vinegar

1. In the slow cooker, mix the almonds, olives, herbs, and oil. Season with salt and pepper.

2. Cover and cook on Low for up to 6 hours. Stir in the vinegar.

3. Serve cool or at room temperature.

Nutritional Highlight: Almonds are rich in protein and dietary fiber. They're also a good source of calcium, magnesium, iron, and vitamin B_6.

Nutritional Information per Serving: Calories: 148; Fat: 14g; Protein: 3g; Carbohydrates: 4g; Sugar: 1g; Sodium: 281mg

Harvard Beets

SERVES 6 TO 8

PREP TIME: 10 MINUTES • COOK TIME: 4 TO 6 HOURS ON LOW

Typically Harvard beets are made with canned beets and drowned in a syrupy, sugary sauce. This version uses fresh beets and a light, honey-sweetened vinaigrette for a healthier take on this classic recipe. They're also delicious when served cold.

2 pounds fresh beets, peeled and
  quartered

2 cups water

½ cup apple cider vinegar

2 tablespoons liquid honey

½ teaspoon sea salt

Freshly ground black pepper

1 tablespoon cornstarch

1. In the slow cooker, mix the beets, water, vinegar, and honey. Season with salt and pepper.

2. Cover and cook on Low for 4 to 6 hours.

3. In a small bowl, whisk together ¼ cup of the cooking liquid and the cornstarch. Pour into the slow cooker, stir, and cook, uncovered, until the sauce is thickened.

Nutritional Highlight: Beets are rich in antioxidants, are anti-inflammatory, and aid the body in detoxification.

Nutritional Information per Serving: Calories: 97; Fat: 0g; Protein: 3g; Carbohydrates: 22g; Sugar: 18g; Sodium: 267mg

THE HEALTHY SLOW COOKER COOKBOOK

Warm Tomato Salad

GLUTEN-FREE **VEGAN** **PALEO-FRIENDLY**

SERVES 4 TO 6

PREP TIME: 5 MINUTES • COOK TIME: 1 TO 2 HOURS ON LOW

This very simple warm summer side dish highlights the beauty of fresh tomatoes. If you can find them, look for heirloom varieties at the supermarket or local farmers' market. Unlike the conventional supermarket tomatoes that have been bred to withstand long transport times and brusque handling, heirloom varieties are a creation of nature. Each one has unique characteristics in color, flavor, and texture, making it a fun journey to explore several varieties at once. Whatever variety of tomato you choose, the slow cooker provides a gentle heat that intensifies tomatoes' flavor and nutrition.

2 pounds tomatoes

½ red onion, very thinly sliced in rings

1 cup fresh basil leaves

2 tablespoons olive oil

Sea salt

Freshly ground black pepper

1. Core the tomatoes. Cut the larger tomatoes in quarters and the medium tomatoes in half, leaving the smaller ones whole. In the slow cooker, mix the tomatoes, onion, basil, and oil. Season generously with salt and pepper.

2. Cover and cook on Low for 1 to 2 hours. (The tomatoes should break down slightly but still be relatively intact.)

Nutritional Highlight: Tomatoes are rich in lycopene, a potent phytochemical that may have anticancer properties. Unlike most other fruits and vegetables, cooking actually improves tomatoes' nutritional composition—cooked tomatoes contain four times as much bioavailable lycopene as raw ones.

Nutritional Information per Serving: Calories: 108; Fat: 8g; Protein: 2g; Carbohydrates: 10g; Sugar: 7g; Sodium: 70mg

Eggplant Caponata

GLUTEN-FREE **VEGAN** **PALEO-FRIENDLY**

SERVES 6 TO 8

PREP TIME: 15 MINUTES • COOK TIME: 8 HOURS ON LOW

Caponata is a Sicilian dish combining eggplants, olives, and onions. It is delicious served over crusty bread and provides a flavorful appetizer rich in fiber, vitamins, minerals, and antioxidants for relatively few calories.

2 medium eggplants, cut into
   1-inch cubes

Sea salt

1 onion, thinly sliced

2 garlic cloves, minced

¼ cup toasted pine nuts

¼ cup dried currants

Pinch red pepper flakes

¼ cup red wine vinegar

1 cup canned tomato sauce or
   Basic Marinara Sauce (page 186)

1 fresh thyme sprig

¼ cup olive oil

1. Sprinkle the eggplant generously with salt and put in a colander for 10 to 15 minutes to drain. Rinse thoroughly under cool running water. Drain well and, using your hands, squeeze excess moisture from the eggplant.

2. In the slow cooker, gently stir together the eggplant, onion, garlic, pine nuts, currants, red pepper flakes, vinegar, tomato sauce, thyme, and oil.

3. Cover and cook on Low for 8 hours.

Tip: Make a batch of caponata early in the week to have on hand for a simple appetizer or snack.

Nutritional Information per Serving: Calories: 180; Fat: 13g; Protein: 3g; Carbohydrates: 17g; Sugar: 9g; Sodium: 257mg

Ginger Carrots

SERVES 6

PREP TIME: 5 MINUTES • COOK TIME: 6 HOURS ON LOW

Most children love carrots, especially when they're cooked until tender and sweet. This is a simple, tasty side dish the whole family will enjoy.

2 pounds baby carrots

½ cup orange juice

1 teaspoon minced fresh ginger

2 tablespoons butter, melted

Sea salt

Freshly ground black pepper

1. In the slow cooker, mix the carrots, orange juice, ginger, and butter. Season with salt and pepper.

2. Cover and cook on Low for 6 hours.

   Variation: For an entirely different but equally delicious flavor, substitute 1 tablespoon of chopped fresh sage for the ginger.

   Nutritional Information per Serving: Calories: 97; Fat: 4g; Protein: 1g; Carbohydrates: 15g; Sugar: 9g; Sodium: 184mg

Southern-Style Collard Greens

GLUTEN-FREE **PALEO-FRIENDLY**

SERVES 6 TO 8

PREP TIME: 10 MINUTES • COOK TIME: 2 HOURS ON HIGH

Collard greens are a Southern tradition, and being a sturdy leafy green, are suited perfectly to cooking in a slow cooker. To prepare collard greens, cut out the thick center rib. Stack the leaves on top of one another, roll lengthwise into a tight cylinder, and, using a sharp knife, cut crosswise into thin slices.

2 slices smoked bacon, diced

1 onion, thinly sliced

4 garlic cloves, minced

2 large bunches collard greens, center ribs removed and cut into long, thin strips

4 cups chicken broth

1 tablespoon apple cider vinegar

Salt

Freshly ground black pepper

2 slices crispy smoked bacon, crumbled into pieces, for garnish (optional)

1. In a large skillet over medium-low heat, cook the bacon with the onion and garlic until softened, about 5 minutes. Transfer mixture to the slow cooker, add the collard greens, and pour in the broth and cider vinegar.

2. Cover and cook on High for 2 hours, or until the greens are bright green and tender. Season with salt and pepper.

3. Serve topped with crumbled bacon (if using).

Nutritional Highlight: You might think vegetable oil is a healthier cooking option than bacon fat, but vegetable oil oxidizes more quickly during cooking than the more heat-stable fat in bacon. Oxidation increases the development of free radicals that will damage your cells. Using the two slices of bacon in this recipe adds a negligible amount of fat per serving but produces a significant amount of flavor.

Nutritional Information per Serving: Calories: 74; Fat: 3g; Protein: 6g; Carbohydrates: 6g; Sugar: 1g; Sodium: 625mg

Mashed Purple Potatoes

GLUTEN-FREE **VEGETARIAN**

SERVES 6 TO 8

PREP TIME: 15 MINUTES • COOK TIME: 6 TO 8 HOURS ON LOW

Purple potatoes have a beautiful dark-colored skin and flesh. They taste similar to yellow-fleshed potatoes but are rich in antioxidants.

2 pounds purple potatoes, peeled

2 cups vegetable broth

½ cup milk

2 tablespoons butter

Sea salt

Freshly ground black pepper

1. In the slow cooker, mix the potatoes and broth.

2. Cover and cook on Low for 6 to 8 hours.

3. Using a potato ricer or potato masher, mash the potatoes just until smooth. Stir in the milk and butter. Season with salt and pepper.

Tip: Be careful not to overwork the potatoes when mashing, or they will become gluey.

Nutritional Information per Serving: Calories: 173; Fat: 5g; Protein: 5g; Carbohydrates: 28g; Sugar: 2g; Sodium: 339mg

Balsamic Root Vegetables

GLUTEN-FREE   **VEGAN**   **PALEO-FRIENDLY**

SERVES 6 TO 8

PREP TIME: 10 MINUTES • COOK TIME: 8 HOURS ON LOW

Potatoes do well in a slow cooker, but there are numerous other root vegetables that offer different flavors, textures, and nutrients. Parsnips, turnips, and carrots combine for a healthy appetizer or side dish.

1 pound parsnips, peeled and quartered

1 pound turnips, peeled and quartered

4 carrots, unpeeled and halved

1 onion, thinly sliced

¼ cup olive oil

¼ cup balsamic vinegar

Sea salt

Freshly ground black pepper

1. In the slow cooker, mix the parsnips, turnips, carrots, and onion.

2. In a small bowl, whisk together the oil and balsamic vinegar. Season generously with salt and pepper. Pour over the vegetables.

3. Cover and cook on Low for 8 hours.

Tip: These vegetables are delicious served as a topping for crusty bread slices along with goat cheese for a healthy appetizer.

Nutritional Information per Serving: Calories: 177; Fat: 9g; Protein: 2g; Carbohydrates: 24g; Sugar: 10g; Sodium: 125mg

Black-Eyed Peas with Rosemary

GLUTEN-FREE · VEGAN

SERVES 4 TO 6

PREP TIME: 5 MINUTES • COOK TIME: 2 TO 4 HOURS ON LOW

Black-eyed peas are rich in dietary fiber and protein, making them a filling side dish, especially for vegetarian diners. Make sure to use the best-quality olive oil you can find; its flavor is prominent in this salad.

2 (15-ounce) cans black-eyed peas, rinsed and drained

½ cup diced onion

1 fresh rosemary sprig, leaves minced

2 tablespoons extra-virgin olive oil

Sea salt

Freshly ground black pepper

¼ cup red wine vinegar

1. In the slow cooker, mix the black-eyed peas, onion, rosemary, and oil. Season with salt and pepper.

2. Cover and cook on Low for 2 to 4 hours.

3. Before serving, stir in the vinegar. Serve warm or chilled.

Variation: This makes a delicious side salad, but you can also make it into a savory dip by blending it in a food processor until almost smooth. Serve with pita triangles or blue corn tortilla chips.

Nutritional Information per Serving: Calories: 227; Fat: 9g; Protein: 11g; Carbohydrates: 30g; Sugar: 1g; Sodium: 103mg

Stuffed Grape Leaves

GLUTEN-FREE **VEGAN**

SERVES 8

PREP TIME: 15 MINUTES • COOK TIME: 4 HOURS ON LOW

This Mediterranean-inspired dish is an impressive and healthy party appetizer. Just make sure to provide plates so guests can set them down between bites. When working with grape leaves, make sure to handle them with care and not to stuff them too full. They should be snug but not tight.

1 cup cooked brown rice

1 teaspoon minced garlic

1 red onion, minced

1 teaspoon minced fresh oregano leaves

1 tablespoon minced fresh parsley leaves

Zest and juice of 1 lemon

Sea salt

Freshly ground black pepper

1 (16-ounce) jar grape leaves, rinsed and drained

½ cup vegetable broth

1. In a small mixing bowl, mix the rice, garlic, onion, herbs, and lemon zest and juice. Season with salt and pepper.

2. Gently separate the individual grape leaves and place them shiny-side down on a clean work surface. Spoon a few tablespoons of the rice mixture onto the leaf. Fold the ends in, then fold in one side and roll until sealed. Place the roll seam-side down in the slow cooker. Repeat with the remaining grape leaves and filling, stacking the rolls on top of each other as needed.

3. Gently pour the vegetable broth into the slow cooker.

4. Cover and cook on Low for 4 hours.

Nutritional Highlight: Grape leaves are a good source of vitamins A and C. They also contain calcium, iron, copper, and manganese.

Nutritional Information per Serving: Calories: 73; Fat: 1g; Protein: 1g; Carbohydrates: 17g; Sugar: 10g; Sodium: 80mg

Apple Sauerkraut with Sausage

GLUTEN-FREE **PALEO-FRIENDLY**

SERVES 6

PREP TIME: 10 MINUTES • COOK TIME: 6 HOURS ON LOW

Chicken sausage has about half the calories and one-third of the fat of pork sausage, making this a guiltless appetizer that's perfect paired with the preceding fondue recipe (page 50) for a healthy Octoberfest party menu.

16 ounces sauerkraut

16 ounces chicken sausage, cut into
  2-inch pieces

3 Granny Smith apples, peeled, cored,
  and diced

Sea salt

Freshly ground black pepper

1 cup apple cider

1. In a colander, rinse the sauerkraut under cool running water. Using your hands, squeeze out excess moisture.

2. Put half of the sauerkraut into the slow cooker. Top with half of the sausage, then half of the diced apples. Repeat those layers, finishing with apples. Season generously with salt and pepper. Pour in the apple cider.

3. Cover and cook on Low for 6 hours.

Tip: Even if you're not normally a fan of sauerkraut, rinsing it first and combining it with sausage and apples mellows its flavor.

Nutritional Information per Serving: Calories: 112; Fat: 2g; Protein: 5g; Carbohydrates: 21g; Sugar: 15g; Sodium: 672mg

Better Buffalo Wings

SERVES 8

PREP TIME: 5 MINUTES • COOK TIME: 3 TO 4 HOURS ON LOW

This classic party appetizer is often drowning in an overly salty sauce and dripping with oil. These wings are a little easier on your waistline, not to mention your supply of napkins, given that they have far less sugar and fat than typical renditions of the classic pub fare.

1 cup hot sauce

2 tablespoons melted butter

1 tablespoon liquid honey

1 teaspoon smoked paprika

1 tablespoon minced garlic

½ cup light beer

Sea salt

2 pounds chicken wings

1. In a bowl, whisk together the hot sauce, butter, honey, paprika, and garlic. Whisk in the beer. Season with salt.

2. Arrange the chicken wings in an even layer in the slow cooker. Pour the buffalo sauce evenly over the wings.

3. Cover and cook on Low for 3 to 4 hours.

Tip: Opt for a hot sauce with few ingredients, low sodium, and no sugar or high-fructose corn syrup.

Nutritional Information per Serving: Calories: 259; Fat: 11g; Protein: 33g; Carbohydrates: 3g; Sugar: 3g; Sodium: 911mg

Korean Short Ribs

SERVES 6 TO 8

PREP TIME: 5 MINUTES • COOK TIME: 8 TO 10 HOURS ON LOW

If you have extra time, marinate the beef up to 4 hours ahead of time to allow all the delicious flavors to meld. If not, don't worry, the slow cooker will keep the meat succulent and flavorful. This recipe uses less sugar and sodium than other versions of Korean short ribs while maintaining all the complex flavors of soy sauce, sesame oil, and rice wine vinegar.

2 tablespoons sesame oil

½ cup soy sauce

2 tablespoons coconut palm sugar
  or brown sugar

2 tablespoons rice wine vinegar

1 tablespoon minced garlic

2 to 3 pounds Korean-style beef short ribs

½ cup thinly sliced scallions

1. In a small bowl, whisk together the sesame oil, soy sauce, sugar, vinegar, and garlic.

2. In the slow cooker, put the beef and top with the scallions. Pour the sauce over the top.

3. Cover and cook on Low for 8 to 10 hours.

Tip: Korean-style ribs can be found in Asian markets. They're cut across the rib bones, resulting in a thinner strip of meat than American-style short ribs.

Nutritional Information per Serving: Calories: 511; Fat: 42g; Protein: 24g; Carbohydrates: 8g; Sugar: 6g; Sodium 1,516mg

Grains and Pastas

Creamy Polenta

GLUTEN-FREE **VEGETARIAN**

MAKES 4 CUPS, 8 SERVINGS

PREP TIME: 5 MINUTES • COOK TIME: 2 HOURS ON LOW

Polenta is a naturally gluten-free, creamy corn-based dish that contains dietary fiber and calcium. Adding just a bit of freshly grated Parmesan ups the calcium and the creamy factor, making this side dish one that your family will request again and again.

7 cups vegetable or chicken broth

1 tablespoon olive oil

2 cups polenta

Sea salt

Freshly ground black pepper

¼ cup freshly grated Parmesan cheese

1. In the slow cooker, mix the broth and oil. Add the polenta in a thin, steady stream, whisking constantly to avoid lumps. Season with salt and pepper.

2. Cover and cook on Low for 2 hours.

3. Stir in the Parmesan just before serving.

Tip: When you're finished with a block of Parmesan, don't throw away the rind! Save it in the freezer along with your other vegetable scraps to make a hearty broth.

Nutritional Information per Serving: Calories: 350; Fat: 7g; Protein: 40g; Carbohydrates: 31g; Sugar: 0g; Sodium: 143mg

Jalapeño Cornbread Dressing

VEGETARIAN

SERVES 6

PREP TIME: 10 MINUTES • COOK TIME: 4 HOURS ON LOW

Making dressing in a slow cooker can be a real help during the holidays when the oven is busy roasting things. Try this savory and slightly spicy cornbread dressing next time you have guests or family coming for dinner.

6 cups cubed cornbread

2 tablespoons butter or olive oil, divided

1 small onion, diced

2 garlic cloves, minced

½ cup canned sliced jalapeños, drained

2 cups chicken or vegetable broth

1. Preheat the oven to 350°F.

2. Spread the cornbread cubes in a single layer on a baking sheet. Bake for 5 minutes, then flip and toast for another 5 minutes.

3. Meanwhile, in a large skillet over medium heat, melt 1 tablespoon of butter. Add the onion and sauté for 5 minutes, until softened. Add the garlic and cook for another minute.

4. Grease the inside of the slow cooker crock with the remaining 1 tablespoon of butter.

5. In the slow cooker, mix the sautéed onion and garlic, bread cubes, and jalapeños. Stir gently to combine. Pour in the broth.

6. Cover and cook on Low for 4 hours.

Variation: Young children might not appreciate the fiery taste of jalapeño peppers. If desired, you can replace them with 1 cup fresh or frozen corn kernels (thawed first if frozen).

Nutritional Information per Serving: Calories: 280; Fat: 10g; Protein: 18g; Carbohydrates: 30g; Sugar: 1g; Sodium: 629mg

Slow Cooker Quinoa

GLUTEN-FREE   VEGAN

SERVES 6

PREP TIME: 5 MINUTES • COOK TIME: 3 TO 4 HOURS ON HIGH

Although quinoa is technically a seed, not a grain, when cooked it has a texture similar to rice. Serve this basic recipe as a healthy side dish or use it as a base for vegetables and cooked meats to build a hearty main dish. While cooking it on the stove top is always faster, using a slow cooker allows you to prepare the dish ahead of time without having to monitor it on the stove.

1 tablespoon olive oil

3 cups vegetable broth

1½ cups quinoa, rinsed and drained

Sea salt

Freshly ground black pepper

1. Grease the inside of the slow cooker crock with the oil.

2. In the slow cooker, mix the broth and quinoa. Season with salt and pepper.

3. Cover and cook on High for 3 to 4 hours, until the quinoa is tender. Fluff with a fork before serving.

Nutritional Highlight: Quinoa is a good source of protein and fiber. It's also rich in manganese, magnesium, iron, copper, and phosphorous. The small amount of olive oil added to this recipe will help your body absorb these and other vitamins and minerals in your meal.

Nutritional Information per Serving: Calories: 187; Fat: 5g; Protein: 8g; Carbohydrates: 26g; Sugar: 0g; Sodium: 423mg

Quinoa and Chicken Sausage Pilaf

GLUTEN-FREE

SERVES 6

PREP TIME: 5 MINUTES • COOK TIME: 3 TO 4 HOURS ON HIGH

Artichoke hearts, sun-dried tomatoes, and chicken sausage are a delicious combination in this hearty pilaf. Enjoy this dish both hot and cold—it makes a lovely summer salad when chilled.

1 tablespoon olive oil

3 cups chicken broth

1½ cups quinoa, rinsed and drained

1 (11-ounce) jar marinated
   artichoke hearts

¼ cup sun-dried tomatoes, minced

1 teaspoon dried oregano

1 link cooked chicken sausage, diced

Sea salt

Freshly ground black pepper

1. Grease the inside of the slow cooker crock with the oil.

2. In the slow cooker, mix the broth, quinoa, artichoke hearts, sun-dried tomatoes, oregano, and sausage. Season with salt and pepper.

3. Cover and cook on High for 3 to 4 hours, until the quinoa is tender. Fluff with a fork before serving.

Tip: You can find chicken sausage in the meat section at your local grocer. It is usually precooked, which means you needn't worry about cooking it long enough in your slow cooker. Simply heat thoroughly and serve.

Nutritional Information per Serving: Calories: 290; Fat: 14g; Protein: 12g; Carbohydrates: 30g; Sugar: 1g; Sodium: 799mg

Mexican Quinoa Casserole

GLUTEN-FREE

SERVES 6

PREP TIME: 10 MINUTES • COOK TIME: 3 TO 4 HOURS ON HIGH

Typically casseroles, which often contain canned ingredients, are one of the least healthy dishes you can make—but it doesn't have to be this way! If you use healthy, whole ingredients and favor fresh flavors, you can create a rich and filling casserole with half the calories, sodium, and saturated fat.

1 tablespoon olive oil

3 cups chicken broth

1½ cups quinoa, rinsed and drained

1 (15-ounce) can red kidney beans, rinsed and drained

1 (15-ounce) can diced fire-roasted tomatoes, with juice

1 teaspoon smoked paprika

1 teaspoon ground cumin

Sea salt

Freshly ground black pepper

2 cups thinly sliced fresh spinach

1 cup shredded sharp Cheddar cheese

½ cup finely chopped fresh cilantro leaves

Lime wedges, for serving

1. Grease the inside of the slow cooker crock with the oil.

2. In the slow cooker, mix the broth, quinoa, beans, tomatoes, and spices. Season with salt and pepper.

3. Cover and cook on High for 3 to 4 hours, until the quinoa is tender.

4. Stir in the spinach, cheese, and cilantro. Cover and cook for another 5 to 10 minutes, or until the cheese is just melted.

5. Serve with lime wedges.

Tip: Quinoa has a naturally bitter coating, so be sure to rinse it under cold running water and drain well before adding it to your recipes.

Nutritional Information per Serving: Calories: 469; Fat: 23g; Protein: 17g; Carbohydrates: 52g; Sugar: 2g; Sodium: 983mg

Roasted Garlic Amaranth

GLUTEN-FREE **VEGAN**

SERVES 4 TO 6

PREP TIME: 5 MINUTES • COOK TIME: 6 TO 8 HOURS ON LOW

Although amaranth is often referred to as a grain, like quinoa, it is actually a seed. It has a mildly nutty taste and, when cooked, a slightly gelatinous texture, which allows it to readily absorb the flavors it's married with. Here we pair it with roasted garlic and thyme for a lovely, rustic side dish.

4 cups chicken or vegetable broth

1½ cups amaranth

1 tablespoon mashed roasted garlic
   (see Tip on page 52)

1 teaspoon fresh thyme leaves

Sea salt

Freshly ground black pepper

1. In the slow cooker, mix the broth, amaranth, garlic, and thyme. Season with salt and pepper.

2. Cover and cook on Low for 6 to 8 hours, until the amaranth is tender.

Nutritional Highlight: Amaranth is rich in protein, particularly the amino acid lysine, which helps our body form collagen and build connective tissues and bones.

Nutritional Information per Serving: Calories: 493; Fat: 9g; Protein: 51g; Carbohydrates: 49g; Sugar: 1g; Sodium: 162mg

Barley Risotto

VEGAN

SERVES 4

PREP TIME: 5 MINUTES • COOK TIME: 4 HOURS ON LOW

Making risotto typically involves standing over a steaming pan of rice, constantly stirring, for half an hour or more. Fortunately, the slow cooker takes all the work out of it and even transforms alternative grains, such as barley, into creamy risotto-like dishes— but with more fiber and protein.

4 cups chicken or vegetable broth

1 cup pearled barley, rinsed

1 leek, white and pale green parts only, finely diced

1 teaspoon fresh thyme leaves

Sea salt

Freshly ground black pepper

¼ cup finely chopped fresh parsley, for serving

1. In the slow cooker, mix the broth, barley, leek, and thyme. Season with salt and pepper.

2. Cover and cook on Low for about 4 hours, or until the barley is tender.

3. Serve topped with the parsley.

Tip: Barley expands while it cooks, so although 1 cup may not seem like a lot, it will after it has absorbed the chicken broth.

Nutritional Information per Serving: Calories: 403; Fat: 5g; Protein: 46g; Carbohydrates: 42g; Sugar: 1g; Sodium: 158mg

Asparagus Risotto

GLUTEN-FREE **VEGETARIAN**

SERVES 4

PREP TIME: 10 MINUTES • COOK TIME: 2 TO 3 HOURS ON HIGH

You might think that risotto is loaded with heavy cream, but it is the starch in the rice that gives the dish its characteristic creaminess. Coupling risotto with fresh asparagus, this side dish offers protein and filling fiber. Serve it alongside broiled salmon for a complete meal.

1½ cups Arborio rice	1 onion, diced
1 tablespoon olive oil	2 garlic cloves, minced
4 cups vegetable broth	Sea salt
½ cup dry white wine	Freshly ground black pepper
2 cups asparagus, cut into 2-inch pieces	½ cup freshly grated Parmesan cheese

1. Pour the rice and oil into the slow cooker. Stir to coat the rice thoroughly. Add the broth, wine, asparagus, onion, and garlic. Season with salt and pepper.

2. Cover and cook on High for 2 to 3 hours, or until the rice is soft but still chewy. Stir in the Parmesan.

Tip: Arborio is a high-starch, short-grain, Italian rice named after the town where it was originally grown. It cooks to a creamy consistency. It is done when it is *al dente* (tender on the outside and firm in the center).

Nutritional Information per Serving: Calories: 423; Fat: 8g; Protein: 16g; Carbohydrates: 65g; Sugar: 3g; Sodium: 961mg

Italian Rice

GLUTEN-FREE **VEGAN**

SERVES 4 TO 6

PREP TIME: 5 MINUTES • COOK TIME: 6 TO 8 HOURS ON LOW

Italy is one of the chief rice-growing regions in Europe, and rice is enjoyed not just in risotto, but also in rice pilafs such as this one. A slow cooker functions similarly to a rice cooker, albeit more slowly, allowing the rice to absorb the liquid and all the delicious flavors.

4 cups chicken or vegetable broth

1½ cups long-grain brown rice

1 tablespoon tomato paste

1 teaspoon minced garlic

1 teaspoon fresh oregano leaves

Sea salt

Freshly ground black pepper

1. In the slow cooker, mix the broth, rice, tomato paste, garlic, and oregano. Season with salt and pepper.

2. Cover and cook on Low for 6 to 8 hours, or until the rice is tender. Fluff with a fork before serving.

Nutritional Highlight: Compared with white rice, brown rice has more than two times the iron, three times the vitamin B_3, four times the vitamin B_1, and ten times the vitamin B_6. It's also loaded with fiber and contains more protein than white rice.

Nutritional Information per Serving: Calories: 475; Fat: 6g; Protein: 46g; Carbohydrates: 56g; Sugar: 1g; Sodium: 154mg

Red Beans and Rice

GLUTEN-FREE **VEGAN**

SERVES 6 TO 8

PREP TIME: 5 MINUTES • COOK TIME: 3 HOURS ON HIGH

It doesn't get any more basic than beans and rice, but coupled with corn, this dish makes a complete protein (see Nutritional Highlight).

4 cups vegetable broth or water

2 cups brown rice

2 cups cooked kidney beans, rinsed and drained

2 cups fresh or frozen corn kernels (thawed if frozen)

1 (15-ounce) can diced fire-roasted tomatoes, with juice

½ cup diced onion

Sea salt

Freshly ground black pepper

1. In the slow cooker, mix the broth, rice, beans, corn, tomatoes, and onion. Season with salt and pepper.

2. Cover and cook on High for 3 hours.

Nutritional Highlight: A complete protein is one that supplies all nine essential amino acids, which are the building blocks of this important macronutrient. Animal sources of protein typically supply all the essential amino acids in appropriate ratios. However, plant sources or protein are often lacking in one or more. For vegans and vegetarians, obtaining adequate protein from a variety of sources will ensure that all amino acids are obtained.

Nutritional Information per Serving: Calories: 517; Fat: 14g; Protein: 14g; Carbohydrates: 88g; Sugar: 4g; Sodium: 1,022mg

Minestrone Soup with Wheat Berries

VEGAN

SERVES 4

PREP TIME: 5 MINUTES • COOK TIME: 8 HOURS ON LOW

With all the talk about the harmful effects of refined grains, skip the processed pasta for your minestrone soup and go with a whole food—wheat berries. The slow cooker allows you to put all the ingredients in in the morning and arrive home to a fully cooked vegan dinner.

1 (28-ounce) can plum tomatoes, with juice

4 cups vegetable broth

1 (15-ounce) can kidney beans, rinsed and drained

2 cups green beans, cut into 2-inch pieces

1 onion, diced

4 garlic cloves, smashed

1½ cups wheat berries

1 tablespoon dried Italian herb blend

Sea salt

Freshly ground black pepper

1. In the slow cooker, mix the tomatoes, broth, beans, onion, garlic, wheat berries, and herbs. Season with salt and pepper.

2. Cover and cook on Low for 8 hours.

Variation: If you prefer fresh herbs, stir in ¼ cup chopped fresh basil and 1 tablespoon chopped fresh oregano just before serving. Cover and cook for 5 minutes to allow the flavors to permeate the broth.

Nutritional Information per Serving: Calories: 287; Fat: 3g; Protein: 17g; Carbohydrates: 52g; Sugar: 13g; Sodium: 1,132mg

Beef and Barley Soup

SERVES 4 TO 6

PREP TIME: 5 MINUTES • COOK TIME: 6 TO 8 HOURS ON LOW

This hearty soup makes a satisfying, warming meal on chilly fall or winter evenings. Serve with a chunk of whole-grain bread and a small side salad.

4 cups beef broth

1 pound top round steak, cut into
   1-inch cubes

1 cup diced carrots

½ cup diced celery

1 onion, diced

½ cup pearl barley

1 teaspoon herbs de Provence

Sea salt

Freshly ground black pepper

1. In the slow cooker, mix the broth, steak, carrots, celery, onion, barley, and herbs de Provence. Season with salt and pepper.

2. Cover and cook on Low for 6 to 8 hours.

Nutritional Highlight: Barley is rich in fiber and has a sweet, nutty flavor. However, it does contain gluten. If you follow a gluten-free diet, consider substituting equal amounts of quinoa or brown rice.

Nutritional Information per Serving: Calories: 396; Fat: 12g; Protein: 44g; Carbohydrates: 26g; Sugar: 4g; Sodium: 924mg

Israeli Couscous with Apricots

VEGAN

SERVES 4

PREP TIME: 5 MINUTES • COOK TIME: 2 HOURS ON LOW

Israeli couscous is similar to standard couscous but is larger and smoother in texture. Choose whole wheat couscous for the most nutrition.

4 cups vegetable broth

1 cup Israeli couscous

½ cup dried apricots, thinly sliced

Zest and juice of 1 orange

Sea salt

Freshly ground black pepper

2 scallions, white and green parts, thinly sliced

1. In the slow cooker, mix the broth, couscous, apricots, and orange zest and juice. Season with salt and pepper.

2. Cover and cook on Low for 2 hours, or until the couscous is tender.

3. Using a fine-mesh sieve, drain any remaining cooking liquid. Return couscous to bowl and stir in the scallions.

Tip: Whole wheat couscous is available at health food markets or in the nutrition aisle of most supermarkets.

Nutritional Information per Serving: Calories: 234; Fat: 2g; Protein: 11g; Carbohydrates: 43g; Sugar: 7g; Sodium: 827mg

Orzo with Spinach and Cranberries

VEGAN

SERVES 4

PREP TIME: 5 MINUTES • COOK TIME: 1 HOUR ON HIGH

Try this sweet and savory side dish when you need something quick and easy. It's equally good when chilled and served as a salad.

4 cups vegetable broth

8 ounces dried orzo pasta

½ cup dried cranberries

Sea salt

Freshly ground black pepper

4 cups fresh spinach, cut into thin slices

Zest and juice of 1 lemon

1. In the slow cooker, mix the broth, orzo, and cranberries. Season with salt and pepper.

2. Cover and cook on High for 1 hour. Stir in the spinach and lemon zest and juice.

3. Serve hot, or refrigerate for 2 hours and serve cold.

Tip: Choose whole wheat orzo pasta for more fiber and protein.

Nutritional Information per Serving: Calories: 214; Fat: 3g; Protein: 12g; Carbohydrates: 35g; Sugar: 1g; Sodium: 486mg

Sage and Pumpkin Mac 'n' Cheese

VEGETARIAN

SERVES 4 TO 6

PREP TIME: 10 MINUTES • COOK TIME: 4 TO 6 HOURS ON LOW

This twist on classic macaroni and cheese replaces much of the cheese with creamy pumpkin or butternut squash, which slashes fat and adds nutrients. If you prefer not to cube the squash yourself, look in the refrigerated case of your produce section for precut squash.

8 ounces dried macaroni noodles

4 cups cubed pumpkin or
  butternut squash

4 cups vegetable broth

1 cup whole milk

1 onion, minced

1 teaspoon fresh thyme leaves

1 tablespoon chopped fresh sage leaves

Sea salt

Freshly ground black pepper

4 ounces fontina cheese, grated

4 ounces pecorino romano cheese, grated

1. In the slow cooker, mix the pasta, pumpkin, broth, milk, onion, and herbs. Season with salt and pepper.

2. Cover and cook on Low for 4 to 6 hours, until pasta is tender.

3. Stir in the cheese, cover, and cook for an additional 10 minutes, or until the cheese is melted.

Nutritional Highlight: Pumpkin is rich in fiber and antioxidants and is the primary food source of alpha-carotene and beta-carotene. It's also rich in vitamins C and B_6, copper, and manganese.

Nutritional Information per Serving: Calories: 582; Fat: 21g; Protein: 32g; Carbohydrates: 67g; Sugar: 10g; Sodium: 1,364mg

Spinach Ravioli in Marinara Sauce

VEGETARIAN

SERVES 4

PREP TIME: 5 MINUTES • COOK TIME: 4 HOURS ON LOW

This vegetarian recipe is perfect for when you're craving lasagna but don't have time to prepare it. Choose whole-grain ravioli for more fiber.

8 cups Basic Marinara Sauce (page 186)

1 (16-ounce) bag fresh spinach ravioli

1 tablespoon dried Italian herb blend

½ cup freshly grated Parmesan cheese

1. In the slow cooker, mix the marinara sauce, ravioli, and herbs. Stir to coat thoroughly. Top with the Parmesan.

2. Cover and cook on Low for 4 hours, or until the ravioli are tender.

Variation: Swap the spinach ravioli for a meat-stuffed ravioli for more protein.

Nutritional Information per Serving: Calories: 395; Fat: 9g; Protein: 18g; Carbohydrates: 57g; Sugar: 13g; Sodium: 763mg

Vegetarian and Vegan Dishes

Vegan Vichyssoise

GLUTEN-FREE **VEGAN**

SERVES 4 TO 6

PREP TIME: 10 MINUTES • COOK TIME: 6 TO 8 HOURS ON LOW

This cool and creamy soup made its mark in America in the early 20th century and is most often attributed to Chef Louis Diat, who recreated a childhood favorite from his upbringing in France. Prepare this soup the night before, cooking it while you sleep. In the morning, simply refrigerate until you're ready to enjoy it.

4 cups vegetable broth

1 pound yellow potatoes, peeled
   and diced

4 leeks, white part only, cut into rings

1 onion, diced

2 fresh thyme sprigs

Sea salt

Freshly ground black pepper

1 cup plain coconut creamer

1. In the slow cooker, mix the broth, potatoes, leeks, onion, and thyme. Season with salt and pepper.

2. Cover and cook on Low for 6 to 8 hours.

3. Discard the thyme sprigs. Using a stand or immersion blender, purée the soup.

4. Stir in the coconut creamer.

5. Set aside to cool slightly, then refrigerate. Serve cold.

Tip: Like many French recipes, the traditional version of vichyssoise relies on copious amounts of cream and butter. This version, however, uses the new coconut-based nondairy creamers for a similar effect. You may use an equal amount of coconut milk or coconut cream, if you wish, but the flavor and texture will not be the same.

Nutritional Information per Serving: Calories: 330; Fat: 16g; Protein: 10g; Carbohydrates: 39g; Sugar: 8g; Sodium: 855mg

Vegan African Peanut Soup

VEGAN

SERVES 4

PREP TIME: 10 MINUTES • COOK TIME: 2 HOURS ON HIGH

This zesty peanut soup is brimming with antioxidants, healthy fats, and fiber. Serve it as an appetizer or enjoy over a bowl of steamed brown rice for a complete meal. For added protein, shred seitan into the soup about 10 minutes before the cooking time is finished.

4 cups vegetable broth

½ cup peanut butter

2 tablespoons tomato paste

1 tablespoon soy sauce

1 bunch collard greens, center ribs removed and roughly chopped

1 onion, diced

1 tablespoon minced fresh ginger

1 tablespoon minced fresh garlic

Sriracha or other Asian hot sauce, for serving

1. In the slow cooker, whisk together the broth, peanut butter, tomato paste, and soy sauce until well combined. Add the collard greens, onion, ginger, and garlic.

2. Cover and cook on High for 2 hours.

3. Serve with Sriracha.

Tip: Want to pack in more vegetables? Add some green and red peppers or carrots to the mix.

Nutritional Information per Serving: Calories: 262; Fat: 18g; Protein: 15g; Carbohydrates: 15g; Sugar: 6g; Sodium: 1,149mg

Broccoli Garlic Tofu

VEGAN

SERVES 2 TO 4

PREP TIME: 15 MINUTES • COOK TIME: 1 TO 2 HOURS ON HIGH

Cooking tofu in a slow cooker allows the tofu time to absorb all the delicious flavors of whatever sauce you happen to cook it in. It also takes all the guesswork out of how to cook this versatile vegetarian protein.

1 block firm tofu

1 cup vegetable broth

2 tablespoons soy sauce

1 tablespoon sesame oil

Juice of 1 lime

1 teaspoon Sriracha or other Asian hot sauce

2 cups broccoli florets

1 tablespoon minced garlic

1. Using a sharp knife, cut the block of tofu crosswise. Put both pieces on a cutting board. Top with a second cutting board and weigh the board down with a heavy skillet or cans of food. Let the tofu drain for about 15 minutes, then cut into 1-inch-thick slices. Put the prepared tofu in a single layer in the slow cooker.

2. In a small bowl, whisk together the broth, soy sauce, sesame oil, lime juice, and Sriracha. Pour over the tofu. Top with the broccoli and garlic.

3. Cover and cook on High for 1 to 2 hours.

Nutritional Highlight: Soy has gone in and out of public favor over the years, but whatever the wind of opinion, enjoy it in moderation and in relatively unprocessed forms. Tofu is rich in protein and is less processed than soy burgers and other faux meat products.

Nutritional Information per Serving: Calories: 158; Fat: 10g; Protein: 10g; Carbohydrates: 10g; Sugar: 2g; Sodium: 1,336mg

Tofu with Mango and Snap Peas

VEGETARIAN

SERVES 4

PREP TIME: 15 MINUTES • COOK TIME: 1 TO 2 HOURS ON HIGH

The creamy sweetness of mango perfectly offsets the savory broth and crunchy snap peas in this Southeast Asian–inspired dish. Serve with steamed rice or atop a generous bed of lettuce.

1 block firm tofu

Juice of 2 limes

¼ cup soy sauce

1 teaspoon liquid honey

Pinch red pepper flakes

4 cups sugar snap peas

1 large mango, peeled and diced

2 plum tomatoes, seeded and diced

½ cup roughly chopped unsalted roasted cashews, for serving

1. Using a sharp knife, cut the block of tofu crosswise. Put both pieces on a cutting board. Top with a second cutting board and weigh the board down with a heavy skillet or cans of food. Let the tofu drain for about 15 minutes, then cut into 1-inch-thick slices. Put the prepared tofu in a single layer in the slow cooker.

2. In a small bowl, whisk together the lime juice, soy sauce, honey, and red pepper flakes. Pour over the tofu. Top with the sugar snap peas.

3. Cover and cook on High for 1 to 2 hours.

4. Just before serving, stir in the mango and tomato. Garnish each serving with cashews.

Tip: More than 90 percent of soybeans grown in the United States are genetically modified. If you have concerns, look for organic and non-GMO tofu, which is fairly easy to find in health food stores.

Nutritional Information per Serving: Calories: 147; Fat: 5g; Protein: 7g; Carbohydrates: 22g; Sugar: 15g; Sodium: 941mg

Barbecue Tofu Burgers

SERVES 4

PREP TIME: 15 MINUTES • COOK TIME: 2 TO 3 HOURS ON LOW

Admit it—barbecue sauce is so delicious, you could enjoy it on just about anything! Tofu works well because it soaks up the smoky, spicy flavors while cooking. Serve it atop whole-grain hamburger buns with a side of fried green tomatoes for a fun summertime vegan supper.

1 block firm tofu

½ cup diced onions

1 garlic clove, minced

2 cups Smoky Barbecue Sauce (page 189)

4 whole-grain hamburger buns, for serving

1 cup shredded lettuce, for serving

1 large tomato, thinly sliced, for serving

1. Using a sharp knife, cut the block of tofu crosswise. Put both pieces on a cutting board. Top with a second cutting board and weigh the board down with a heavy skillet or cans of food. Let the tofu drain for about 15 minutes, then cut into cubes. Put the prepared tofu in a single layer in the slow cooker. Top with the onions and garlic, then pour in the barbecue sauce.

2. Cover and cook on Low for 2 to 3 hours.

3. Serve on hamburger buns with lettuce and tomato.

Nutritional Information per Serving: Calories: 249; Fat: 3g; Protein: 10g; Carbohydrates: 53g; Sugar: 25g; Sodium: 1,390mg

Orange-Glazed Tempeh and Green Beans

VEGAN

SERVES 4

PREP TIME: 5 MINUTES • COOK TIME: 4 HOURS ON LOW

Tempeh is made from fermented soybeans and contains a whopping 31 grams of protein per cup. Most of the soy eaten in Asian countries, where it has been found to have numerous health benefits, is fermented. Other fermented soy products include miso and soy sauce.

8 ounces tempeh, cut into 2-inch slices

1 pound green beans, trimmed

1 cup orange juice

1 tablespoon soy sauce

1 tablespoon coconut sugar or brown sugar

1 teaspoon finely grated orange zest

Rice or rice noodles, for serving

1. In the slow cooker, mix the tempeh, green beans, orange juice, soy sauce, sugar, and orange zest.

2. Cover and cook on Low for 4 hours.

3. Serve over rice or rice noodles.

Nutritional Highlight: Fermented soy may be more easily digestible than soy milk, tofu, and especially the isolated soy protein used in many vegetarian meat replacements.

Nutritional Information per Serving: Calories: 184; Fat: 6g; Protein: 13g; Carbohydrates: 23g; Sugar: 9g; Sodium: 239mg

Tempeh Tacos

VEGETARIAN

SERVES 4

PREP TIME: 5 MINUTES • COOK TIME: 1 TO 2 HOURS ON LOW

When crumbled, tempeh bears a surprising resemblance to ground beef, especially when it's smothered in all the spices and sauce of traditional taco filling.

16 ounces tempeh, crumbled

1 onion, minced

2 garlic cloves, minced

1 tablespoon ground cumin

1 teaspoon smoked paprika

¼ teaspoon cayenne pepper

1 cup tomato ketchup

Sea salt

Freshly ground black pepper

8 whole wheat tortillas, for serving

1 cup shredded cheese, for serving

2 cups shredded lettuce, for serving

½ cup sour cream, for serving

1. In the slow cooker, mix the tempeh, onion, garlic, spices, and ketchup. Season with salt and pepper.

2. Cover and cook on Low for 1 to 2 hours.

3. To serve, fill each tortilla with about ⅓ cup tempeh filling. Top with shredded cheese, lettuce, and sour cream.

Tip: Tempeh also works well crumbled in marinara sauce as a stand-in for other protein options. It also browns nicely when panfried in a bit of oil.

Nutritional Information per Serving: Calories: 698; Fat: 30g; Protein: 39g; Carbohydrates: 76g; Sugar: 15g; Sodium: 1,344mg

Mushroom Cassoulet

GLUTEN-FREE **VEGAN**

SERVES 4

PREP TIME: 10 MINUTES • COOK TIME: 8 HOURS ON LOW

Traditionally, cassoulet is made with pork. This vegetarian version substitutes a combination of fresh and dried mushrooms and herbs to achieve a similar rich, rustic flavor.

2 (15-ounce) cans navy beans, rinsed and drained

2 cups vegetable broth

2 ounces dried wild mushrooms

2 cups cremini or button mushrooms

1 cup diced carrots

1 cup diced onions

1 cup diced celery

1 tablespoon herbs de Provence

Sea salt

Freshly ground black pepper

1. In the slow cooker, mix the beans, broth, mushrooms, carrots, onions, celery, and herbs de Provence. Season with salt and pepper.

2. Cover and cook on Low for 8 hours.

Nutritional Highlight: A study conducted in 2007 by Johns Hopkins Bloomberg School of Public Health found that replacing meat entrées with mushroom-based entrées at lunchtime resulted in a net reduction of 300 calories at that meal and another 300 fewer calories consumed later in the day.

Nutritional Information per Serving: Calories: 298; Fat: 2g; Protein: 21g; Carbohydrates: 52g; Sugar: 5g; Sodium: 1,438mg

Italian Stuffed Peppers

GLUTEN-FREE **VEGETARIAN**

SERVES 4

PREP TIME: 10 MINUTES • COOK TIME: 2 HOURS ON HIGH OR 6 HOURS ON LOW

If you're craving lasagna but want a low-carb option, try these stuffed peppers. They have all the flavors of a traditional lasagna, but without the noodles, which makes them naturally gluten-free, too.

1 teaspoon olive oil

4 red peppers, cored

1 cup cottage cheese

1 cup shredded Italian cheese blend

¼ cup minced fresh basil leaves

1 teaspoon dried Italian herb blend

1 egg, whisked

¼ cup freshly grated Parmesan cheese

1. Lightly grease the inside of the slow cooker with the oil. Arrange the cored peppers inside. (You may wish to slice a small portion off of the bottom of each pepper to help them stand up, but be careful not to make a hole that would allow the filling to escape.)

2. In a small mixing bowl, whisk together the cottage cheese, shredded Italian cheese, herbs, and egg. Spoon the mixture evenly into the peppers. Sprinkle each pepper with Parmesan.

3. Cover and cook on High for 2 hours or on Low for 6 hours.

Tip: If fresh basil isn't in season, double the amount of dried Italian herb blend used.

Nutritional Information per Serving: Calories: 223; Fat: 14g; Protein: 19g; Carbohydrates: 7g; Sugar: 3g; Sodium: 532mg

Quinoa-Stuffed Tomatoes

GLUTEN-FREE **VEGETARIAN**

SERVES 4

PREP TIME: 10 MINUTES • COOK TIME: 4 HOURS ON LOW

Sometimes you just want to round up the leftovers in your refrigerator and use them up all at one time. This dish is perfect for the job.

4 large tomatoes (preferably Beefsteak), stemmed, seeded, and cored

Sea salt

1 cup cooked quinoa

1 cup diced vegetables, such as carrots, zucchini, or spinach

1 garlic clove, minced

1 teaspoon dried Italian herb blend

Freshly ground black pepper

1 teaspoon olive oil

¼ cup freshly grated Parmesan cheese

1. Sprinkle the inside of each tomato with salt, then put upside down in a colander to drain.

2. Meanwhile, in a small mixing bowl, mix the quinoa, vegetables, garlic, and herbs, and season with salt and pepper. Spoon the mixture evenly into the tomatoes.

3. Lightly grease the inside of the slow cooker with olive oil. Put the tomatoes inside and sprinkle each with Parmesan.

4. Cover and cook on Low for 4 hours.

Tip: When choosing tomatoes, opt for firm, ripe fruits. They will hold up best during the long, slow cooking if they're more robust.

Nutritional Information per Serving: Calories: 142; Fat: 4g; Protein: 7g; Carbohydrates: 21g; Sugar: 5g; Sodium: 589mg

Vegetarian Quinoa Paella

GLUTEN-FREE   VEGAN

SERVES 4

PREP TIME: 10 MINUTES • COOK TIME: 6 TO 8 HOURS ON LOW

While this isn't a traditional paella with chorizo and fresh shrimp, it does capture the flavors of Spain in every mouthful. Quinoa bumps up the nutrients, and vegan chorizo sausage has half the calories of the cured meat version and almost no saturated fat.

4 cups vegetable broth

1 (15-ounce) can diced fire-roasted
   tomatoes, with juice

1½ cups quinoa, rinsed and drained

6 ounces vegan chorizo sausage, diced

1 onion, diced

1 fennel bulb, quartered, cored, and
   thinly sliced

Pinch Spanish saffron (optional)

1 cup frozen peas, thawed

1 tablespoon minced fresh parsley leaves

1. In the slow cooker, mix the broth, tomatoes, quinoa, sausage, onion, fennel, and saffron (if using).

2. Cover and cook on Low for 6 to 8 hours.

3. Stir in the peas and parsley and cook until just heated through, about 5 minutes.

Tip: If you don't have any saffron on hand, a pinch of turmeric will lend the same golden color.

Nutritional Information per Serving: Calories: 173; Fat: 4g; Protein: 8g; Carbohydrates: 27g; Sugar: 6g; Sodium: 139mg

Cuban Black Beans

GLUTEN-FREE **VEGAN**

SERVES 8

PREP TIME: 10 MINUTES • COOK TIME: 4 TO 6 HOURS ON LOW

The secret to succulent Cuban-style black beans is long, slow cooking, which makes this recipe perfectly suited to the slow cooker. Enjoy these hearty beans with steamed brown rice and a generous dollop of fresh guacamole.

2 (15-ounce) cans black beans (do not rinse or drain)

4 scallions, white and green parts, roughly chopped

½ green pepper, diced

4 garlic cloves, minced

1 tablespoon ground cumin

1 bay leaf

Sea salt

Freshly ground black pepper

1. In the slow cooker, mix the beans, scallions, green pepper, garlic, cumin, and bay leaf. Season with salt and pepper.

2. Cover and cook on Low for 4 to 6 hours. Discard the bay leaf before serving.

Tip: Some people find dried beans more easily digestible. To use dried beans in this recipe, you need to soak and cook them first: In a bowl, cover beans in unsalted water and set aside overnight. Rinse and drain. Transfer beans to a saucepan, cover with unsalted water, and simmer over medium heat for at least 1 hour before proceeding with the recipe as written. Beans contain natural toxins that are neutralized by cooking at high temperatures, which is why most of the recipes in this book use canned beans.

Nutritional Information per Serving: Calories: 105; Fat: 1g; Protein: 7g; Carbohydrates: 18g; Sugar: 0g; Sodium: 47mg

Moroccan Lentils

GLUTEN-FREE **VEGAN**

SERVES 5

PREP TIME: 10 MINUTES • COOK TIME: 4 HOURS ON HIGH OR 8 HOURS ON LOW

All the flavors of Morocco come together in this savory side dish. Enjoy with a glass of refreshing mint tea, crusty bread, and a generous salad.

4 cups vegetable broth

1 (15-ounce) can diced tomatoes,
 with juice

1 cup red lentils

1 onion, diced

2 or 3 carrots, diced

2 garlic cloves, minced

1 teaspoon ground ginger

1 teaspoon ground cumin

½ teaspoon ground turmeric

½ teaspoon ground cinnamon

½ teaspoon ground coriander

Zest and juice of 1 lemon

Sea salt

Freshly ground black pepper

1. In the slow cooker, mix the broth, tomatoes, lentils, onion, carrots, garlic, ginger, cumin, turmeric, cinnamon, coriander, and lemon zest and juice. Season with salt and pepper.

2. Cover and cook on High for 4 hours or on Low for 8 hours.

Nutritional Highlight: Lentils are an excellent source of dietary fiber and protein. They also contain generous amounts of vitamins and minerals, including folate, copper, phosphorous, iron, potassium, vitamins B_1 and B_6, and zinc.

Nutritional Information per Serving: Calories: 207; Fat: 2g; Protein: 15g; Carbohydrates: 33g; Sugar: 6g; Sodium: 682mg

Lentil Chili

GLUTEN-FREE **VEGAN**

SERVES 4 TO 6

PREP TIME: 10 MINUTES • COOK TIME: 4 HOURS ON HIGH OR 6 HOURS ON LOW

Why should beans get all the fun in vegetarian versions of chili? In this recipe, black beans play second fiddle to lentils.

4 cups vegetable broth

2 cups red lentils

1 (15-ounce) can diced fire-roasted
   tomatoes, with juice

1 (15-ounce) can black beans, rinsed
   and drained (see Tip on page 101)

2 yellow or red peppers, cored and diced

1 onion, diced

2 tablespoons chili powder

1 tablespoon ground cumin

1 teaspoon smoked paprika

1 avocado, sliced, for serving

1 cup loosely packed fresh cilantro leaves,
   for serving

1. In the slow cooker, mix the broth, lentils, tomatoes, beans, yellow peppers, onion, chili powder, cumin, and paprika.

2. Cover and cook on High for 4 hours or on Low for 6 hours.

3. Serve with sliced avocado and fresh cilantro.

Nutritional Highlight: While this dish is naturally low in fat, your body needs some fat to help absorb the nutrients. So, pile on that avocado. It's rich in monounsaturated fats, which help reduce central abdominal fat.

Nutritional Information per Serving: Calories: 682; Fat: 14g; Protein: 42g; Carbohydrates: 100g; Sugar: 8g; Sodium: 1,051mg

Spanish Chickpeas and Spinach

GLUTEN-FREE **VEGAN**

SERVES 2 TO 4

PREP TIME: 10 MINUTES • COOK TIME: 6 TO 8 HOURS ON LOW

This dish is a vegan one-pot wonder. It's rich in complex carbohydrates, fiber, and protein with next to no fat.

2 cups vegetable broth

1 cup quinoa, rinsed and drained

1 (15-ounce) can chickpeas, rinsed
  and drained

16 ounces frozen spinach, thawed and
  squeezed of excess liquid

2 tablespoons olive oil

2 tablespoons red wine or sherry vinegar

1 tablespoon smoked paprika

1 teaspoon ground cumin

Sea salt

Freshly ground black pepper

2 plum tomatoes, diced

1. In the slow cooker, mix the broth and quinoa. Top with the chickpeas and spinach.

2. In a measuring cup, whisk together the oil, vinegar, and spices. Season with salt and pepper. Pour the mixture over the contents of the slow cooker.

3. Cover and cook on Low for 6 to 8 hours.

4. Just before serving, stir in the tomatoes.

Tip: Smoked paprika and sherry vinegar are quintessential ingredients in Spanish cuisine. They're loaded with flavor and easy to find in well-stocked markets.

Nutritional Information per Serving: Calories: 654; Fat: 18g; Protein: 41g; Carbohydrates: 105g; Sugar: 8g; Sodium: 1,205mg

Coconut and Chickpea Curry

GLUTEN-FREE **VEGAN**

SERVES 4

PREP TIME: 5 MINUTES • COOK TIME: 8 HOURS ON LOW

This simple yellow curry is rich in healthy fats, filling fiber, vitamins, and minerals. It's amazing on its own or served with steamed jasmine rice.

2 (15-ounce) cans chickpeas, drained and rinsed

1 (15-ounce) can coconut milk

1 cup diced onion

½ cup diced yellow or red pepper

2 minced garlic cloves

1 teaspoon grated ginger root

1 teaspoon garam masala

1 teaspoon ground coriander

1 teaspoon kosher salt

½ teaspoon ground turmeric

½ teaspoon ground cumin

½ teaspoon freshly ground black pepper

¼ teaspoon ground cayenne pepper, optional

½ cup toasted, unsweetened coconut shreds for garnish

1. In the slow cooker, mix the chickpeas, coconut milk, onion, peppers, garlic, ginger, salt, and remaining spices.

2. Cover and cook on Low for 8 hours.

3. Serve sprinkled with toasted coconut shreds.

Nutritional Highlight: Turmeric is a natural anti-inflammatory and what gives curry powder its brilliant yellow hue. Turmeric is also a potent antioxidant, which means it neutralizes the oxidative, or cell-damaging, effects of a poor diet, environmental toxins, and stress.

Nutritional Information per Serving: Calories: 688; Fat: 35g; Protein: 24g; Carbohydrates: 76g; Sugar: 17g; Sodium: 628mg

Indian Chickpeas with Yogurt and Cardamom

GLUTEN-FREE **VEGETARIAN**

SERVES 4

PREP TIME: 5 MINUTES • COOK TIME: 6 TO 8 HOURS ON LOW

This protein- and fiber-rich entrée is delicious served over rice or quinoa or with naan.

2 teaspoons garam masala

1 teaspoon ground cumin

1 teaspoon ground coriander

1 teaspoon ground ginger

¼ teaspoon ground cardamom

½ teaspoon ground cinnamon

2 (15-ounce) cans chickpeas, rinsed
     and drained

2 cups vegetable broth

1 onion, diced

2 garlic cloves, minced

Sea salt

Freshly ground black pepper

1 large tomato, seeded and diced

4 cups fresh spinach, cut into thin slices

1 cup plain full-fat yogurt

Fresh cilantro, for serving

1. In a small mixing bowl, whisk together all the spices until well combined.

2. In the slow cooker, mix the prepared spice blend, chickpeas, broth, onion, and garlic. Season with salt and pepper.

3. Cover and cook on Low for 6 to 8 hours. Allow to rest, uncovered, for about 10 minutes before serving.

4. Stir in the tomato, spinach, and yogurt. Garnish with fresh cilantro.

Tip: If you don't happen to have all these spices in your pantry, check out the bulk spice section of your local market. You won't have to splurge on full bottles of spices.

Nutritional Information per Serving: Calories: 287; Fat: 4g; Protein: 21g; Carbohydrates: 42g; Sugar: 4g; Sodium: 491mg

Fiery Seitan Fajitas

VEGAN

SERVES 4

PREP TIME: 10 MINUTES • COOK TIME: 4 HOURS ON LOW

Sure, fiery seitan sounds a little ominous, but you'll be in spicy food heaven when you try these juicy vegan tacos.

8 ounces seitan, roughly chopped

1 cup canned tomato sauce or
    Basic Marinara Sauce (page 186)

½ cup hot sauce

½ cup minced onion

1 small green pepper, diced

1 tablespoon smoked paprika

1 tablespoon ground cumin

¼ teaspoon sea salt

8 corn tortillas, for serving

Avocado slices, for serving

Lime wedges, for serving

1. In the slow cooker, mix the seitan, tomato sauce, hot sauce, onion, green pepper, paprika, cumin, and salt.

2. Cover and cook on Low for 4 hours.

3. Serve in corn tortillas with avocado slices and lime wedges.

Nutritional Highlight: Seitan is about as opposite of the gluten-free diet as you could ever get. This vegan protein source is made from nothing but gluten. Its texture is one of the closest vegetarian replications of chicken.

Nutritional Information per Serving: Calories: 472; Fat: 15g; Protein: 48g; Carbohydrates: 33g; Sugar: 5g; Sodium: 2,127mg

Seitan "Stir-Fry"

SERVES 4

PREP TIME: 10 MINUTES • COOK TIME: 2 HOURS ON HIGH

This is the slow cooker's version of a stir-fry: fresh vegetables combined with seitan (for protein) and a tasty sauce. It's perfect for "meatless Mondays" or any time you want to enjoy a vegetarian meal.

8 ounces seitan, roughly chopped

1 cup vegetable broth

½ cup soy sauce

2 tablespoons lime juice

2 red peppers, thinly sliced

2 carrots, thinly sliced

1 onion, cut into rings

1 teaspoon minced garlic

Pinch red pepper flakes

Steamed rice or rice noodles, for serving

1. In the slow cooker, mix the seitan, broth, soy sauce, lime juice, red peppers, carrots, onion, garlic, and red pepper flakes.

2. Cover and cook on High for 2 hours.

3. Serve over steamed rice or rice noodles.

Tip: To save time, look for precut vegetables in the refrigerated section of the produce department.

Nutritional Information per Serving: Calories: 293; Fat: 3g; Protein: 47g; Carbohydrates: 12g; Sugar: 5g; Sodium: 360mg

Three-Cheese Lasagna

VEGETARIAN

SERVES 6 TO 8

PREP TIME: 15 MINUTES • COOK TIME: 4 HOURS ON LOW

This may be the best lasagna recipe you ever try, and it doesn't have a shred of meat in it. All the flavor, not to mention a generous 25 grams of protein per serving, comes from a blend of cheeses and a very generous amount of fresh basil.

8 cups prepared marinara sauce or Basic Marinara Sauce (page 186)

1 cup finely chopped onion

1 tablespoon minced garlic

1 tablespoon coarsely ground fennel seed

Pinch red pepper flakes

1 tablespoon olive oil

16 ounces lasagna noodles, cooked according to package directions

16 ounces cottage cheese

16 ounces mozzarella cheese, divided

8 ounces freshly grated Parmesan cheese

2 eggs

2 cups roughly chopped fresh basil leaves, divided

1. In a bowl, mix the marinara sauce, onion, garlic, fennel, red pepper flakes, and oil. Ladle about ½ cup of the mixture into the bottom of the slow cooker (enough to thoroughly coat the bottom of the slow cooker crock).

2. Arrange a layer of lasagna noodles on the bottom of the slow cooker crock, allowing them to rise up the sides of the crock slightly. Trim as needed. Ladle additional marinara sauce over them.

3. In a large mixing bowl, mix the cottage cheese, all but ½ cup of the mozzarella cheese, Parmesan, and eggs. Layer about half of the cheese mixture on top of the noodles. Top with 1 cup of basil.

4. Repeat with a layer of pasta, marinara sauce, the remainder of the cheese mixture, and the remaining 1 cup of basil.

5. Finish with the remaining pasta, marinara sauce, and reserved ½ cup mozzarella cheese. ▶

6. Cover and cook on Low for 4 hours.

7. Allow to rest, uncovered, for at least 15 minutes before serving.

Variation: Feel free to use other varieties of cheese instead of the mozzarella and Parmesan. Some flavorful options include Asiago, pecorino, fontina, and Grana Padano. If you're concerned about the amount of fat, feel free to swap out some of the cheese for shredded zucchini or shredded mixed vegetables.

Nutritional Information per Serving: Calories: 835; Fat: 30g; Protein: 63g; Carbohydrates: 81g; Sugar: 23g; Sodium: 2,285mg

Vegetarian Quiche

GLUTEN-FREE **VEGETARIAN**

SERVES 4

PREP TIME: 20 MINUTES • COOK TIME: 8 HOURS ON LOW

This quiche is an easy way to sneak vegetables into breakfast and is incredibly versatile—use whatever combination of vegetables you prefer.

1 tablespoon butter

2 cups fresh spinach leaves, shredded

1 cup grape tomatoes, halved

1 tablespoon chopped fresh herbs,
    such as chives or parsley

½ cup Italian blend shredded cheese

6 eggs

½ cup milk

Sea salt

Freshly ground black pepper

1. Butter the inside of the slow cooker crock.

2. In the slow cooker, gently mix the spinach, tomatoes, herbs, and cheese.

3. In a bowl, whisk together the eggs and milk and season with salt and pepper. Pour over the vegetable mixture and stir gently to combine. Cook on Low for 8 hours.

Variation: For a traditional breakfast casserole, add 2 cups of cubed whole wheat bread to the bottom of the slow cooker before adding the vegetable mixture. You'll get more fiber and may feel fuller longer.

Nutritional Information per Serving: Calories: 191; Fat: 14g; Protein: 14g; Carbohydrates: 4g; Sugar: 3g; Sodium: 295mg

Fish and Shellfish

■ ■ ■ ■ ■ ■ ■ ■ ■ ■ ■ ■ ■ ■ ■ ■ ■ ■ ■

Shrimp Fajitas

SERVES 4 TO 6

PREP TIME: 10 MINUTES • COOK TIME: 1 TO 2 HOURS PLUS 15 MINUTES ON HIGH

Enjoy this fajita filling with whole wheat tortillas or, for a more authentic preparation, with small corn tortillas.

1 green pepper, sliced

2 yellow, red, or orange peppers, sliced

2 onions, halved and thinly sliced

2 tablespoons olive oil

1 tablespoon ground cumin

¼ teaspoon cayenne pepper

Sea salt

Freshly ground black pepper

½ cup white wine

2 pounds shrimp, peeled and deveined

1. In the slow cooker, mix the peppers, onions, and oil. Add the cumin and cayenne, season with salt and pepper, and stir to combine.

2. Cover and cook on High for 1 to 2 hours.

3. Add the white wine and shrimp. Cover and cook for another 15 minutes, or until the shrimp are cooked through.

Nutritional Highlight: Shrimp are an excellent source of protein, containing 24 grams per serving.

Nutritional Information per Serving: Calories: 272; Fat: 8g; Protein: 36g; Carbohydrates: 10g; Sugar: 4g; Sodium: 413mg

THE HEALTHY SLOW COOKER COOKBOOK

Shrimp Scampi with Orzo

SERVES 4

PREP TIME: 5 MINUTES • COOK TIME: 1 TO 2 HOURS ON LOW

This one-dish meal is easy to prepare in the slow cooker, leaving you free to do other things while it cooks. Use whole wheat orzo to keep this dish healthy and rich in fiber and protein.

1 tablespoon butter

1 pound shrimp, peeled and deveined

1 cup whole wheat orzo pasta

¼ cup minced fresh parsley

2 teaspoons minced garlic

4 cups chicken broth

½ cup dry white wine

Sea salt

Freshly ground black pepper

1. Butter the inside of the slow cooker crock.

2. In the slow cooker, mix the shrimp, pasta, parsley, and garlic. Pour in the broth and wine. Season with salt and pepper.

3. Cover and cook on Low for 1 to 2 hours, or until the pasta is tender and the shrimp is cooked through.

Tip: The Monterey Bay Aquarium, which provides an annual Seafood Watch for the healthiest, most environmentally sustainable seafood options, recommends purchasing freshwater shrimp from the United States or spot shrimp from Canada. It advises against imported black tiger and white shrimp as well as Pacific white and West Coast white shrimp from Mexico.

Nutritional Information per Serving: Calories: 422; Fat: 7g; Protein: 38g; Carbohydrates: 43g; Sugar: 1g; Sodium: 1,123mg

Clams in White Wine Butter Sauce

GLUTEN-FREE

SERVES 4

PREP TIME: 10 MINUTES • COOK TIME: 40 MINUTES ON HIGH

Clams in wine and butter sauce is ubiquitous on appetizer menus around the world. Unfortunately, it's typically loaded with added fat and salt. This recipe uses a fraction of the butter typically used in restaurants and instead relies on quality seafood and fresh herbs for its fantastic flavor.

4 tablespoons cold butter, divided

1 cup chicken or vegetable broth

1 cup dry white wine

¼ cup minced shallots

1 teaspoon fresh thyme leaves

2 garlic cloves, minced

Juice of 1 lemon

Sea salt

Freshly ground black pepper

2 pounds fresh clams, scrubbed
    and debearded

Fresh flat-leaf parsley, for serving

1. Butter the inside of the slow cooker crock with 1 tablespoon butter.

2. In the slow cooker, mix the broth, wine, shallots, thyme, garlic, and lemon juice. Season with salt and pepper. Gently add the clams.

3. Cover and cook on High for 30 minutes, or until nearly all the clams have opened. Discard any that do not open.

4. Transfer the clams to a serving platter. Continue to cook the sauce, uncovered, for another 10 minutes on High. (It should reduce somewhat.) Whisk in the remaining 3 tablespoons of butter, 1 tablespoon at a time, to thicken the sauce. Carefully pour over the clams and garnish with the parsley.

Tip: If you want to lighten things up, omit the 3 tablespoons of butter added at the end of the cooking process and simply reduce the sauce for another 5 minutes before pouring over the cooked clams.

Nutritional Information per Serving: Calories: 323; Fat: 13g; Protein: 12g; Carbohydrates: 29g; Sugar: 8g; Sodium: 988mg

Mussels in Saffron Curry Sauce

GLUTEN-FREE **PALEO-FRIENDLY**

SERVES 4

PREP TIME: 10 MINUTES • COOK TIME: 30 MINUTES ON LOW

The combination of saffron and curry gives these mussels an Eastern flavor. Serve with steamed rice or as an appetizer with toasted whole-grain bread.

1 tablespoon butter

2 cups chicken broth

1 cup vermouth

½ cup diced onion

2 plum tomatoes, diced

2 garlic cloves, minced

1 bay leaf

1 teaspoon curry powder

Pinch saffron threads (optional)

1 lemon, halved

Sea salt

Freshly ground black pepper

2 pounds fresh mussels, scrubbed
   and debearded

¼ cup roughly chopped flat-leaf parsley,
   for serving

1. Butter the inside of the slow cooker crock.

2. In the slow cooker, mix the broth, vermouth, onion, tomatoes, garlic, and bay leaf. Stir in the curry powder, saffron (if using), and lemon halves. Season with salt and pepper.

3. Gently add the mussels to the broth mixture.

4. Cover and cook on Low for 30 minutes, or until the mussels open. Discard any mussels that remain closed and the bay leaf. Serve sprinkled with chopped parsley.

Nutritional Highlight: A 3-ounce serving of mussels contains an impressive 340 percent of your daily recommended value of vitamin B_{12}. This critical nutrient keeps the body's nerve and blood cells healthy. It's also crucial in maintaining healthy energy levels.

Nutritional Information per Serving: Calories: 320; Fat: 9g; Protein: 31g; Carbohydrates: 16g; Sugar: 4g; Sodium: 1,120mg

Seared Scallops over Stewed Collards and Beans

SERVES 4

PREP TIME: 5 MINUTES • COOK TIME: 1 HOUR PLUS 15 TO 30 MINUTES ON HIGH

Scallops are rich in protein, and when paired with stewed collard greens and cooked beans, they make a complete one-dish meal.

1 bunch collard greens

1 (15-ounce) can cannellini beans,
   rinsed and drained

1 tablespoon olive oil

Sea salt

Freshly ground black pepper

1 pound sea scallops

Zest and juice of 1 lemon

1. To prepare the collard greens, remove and discard the tough center ribs. Stack the leaves and roll into a tight cylinder. Using a sharp knife, make thin, perpendicular cuts to create a rough chiffonade.

2. In the slow cooker, mix the collard greens, beans, and oil. Season with salt and pepper.

3. Cover and cook on High for 1 hour, or until the greens are bright and somewhat tender.

4. Add the scallops and lemon zest and juice, and cook for another 15 to 30 minutes, or until the scallops are opaque and cooked through.

Tip: To increase the flavor of this dish, pat the scallops dry and season generously with salt and pepper. Sear in a very hot skillet with a small amount of butter or olive oil for about 1 minute on each side to form a crust. Add to the slow cooker and cook for about 15 minutes.

Nutritional Information per Serving: Calories: 225; Fat: 5g; Protein: 25g; Carbohydrates: 21g; Sugar: 2g; Sodium: 638mg

Mediterranean
Poached Halibut

GLUTEN-FREE **PALEO-FRIENDLY**

SERVES 4

PREP TIME: 10 MINUTES • COOK TIME: 1 HOUR ON HIGH

The Mediterranean diet has long been recognized as heart healthy and praised for increasing longevity. It tastes pretty good, too. In this dish, the capers and herbs provide complex flavors with virtually no added calories or sodium.

2 tablespoons olive oil

1 (15-ounce) can whole plum tomatoes, with juice

¼ cup capers, drained

2 zucchini, julienned

2 garlic cloves, roughly chopped

1 cup fresh basil leaves, divided

1 teaspoon herbs de Provence

Sea salt

Freshly ground black pepper

4 (4-ounce) halibut fillets

1. Grease the inside of the slow cooker crock with the oil.

2. In the slow cooker, mix the tomatoes, capers, zucchini, garlic, half of the basil, and the herbs de Provence. Season with salt and pepper. Top with the halibut fillets.

3. Cover and cook on High for 1 hour, or until the fish flakes easily with a fork.

4. Serve garnished with the remaining ½ cup of basil.

Tip: To julienne vegetables or hard fruits such as apples, use a sharp chef's knife to cut very thin slices, then stack the slices on top of one another, about 1 to 2 inches thick, and slice into very thin slivers.

Nutritional Information per Serving: Calories: 426; Fat: 14g; Protein: 63g; Carbohydrates: 10g; Sugar: 4g; Sodium: 497mg

Halibut in Mango Pineapple Chutney

GLUTEN-FREE **PALEO-FRIENDLY**

SERVES 4

PREP TIME: 10 MINUTES • COOK TIME: 4 TO 6 HOURS ON LOW

Enjoy the flavors of India in this spicy curried chutney. Many chutney recipes call for added sugar, but the mango and pineapple bring plenty of sweetness to this dish, so why add empty calories from refined sugar?

1 cup diced fresh pineapple

2 large mangos, peeled and diced

2 tomatoes, seeded and diced

1 red onion, diced

1 teaspoon curry powder

1 teaspoon ground ginger

1 teaspoon ground coriander

½ cup red wine vinegar

Sea salt

Freshly ground black pepper

4 (4-ounce) halibut fillets

1. In the slow cooker, mix the pineapple, mangos, tomatoes, onion, curry powder, ginger, and coriander. Pour in the red wine vinegar and stir to combine. Season with salt and pepper.

2. Cover and cook on Low for 4 to 6 hours.

3. In the last 30 minutes of cooking, add the halibut, cover, and cook until the fish flakes easily with a fork.

Tip: If you're serving this dish to young children, you may want to consider reducing the amount of curry powder to ¼ teaspoon.

Nutritional Information per Serving: Calories: 443; Fat: 7g; Protein: 62g; Carbohydrates: 29g; Sugar: 22g; Sodium: 222mg

Lemon-Poached Cod
with Chimichurri

GLUTEN-FREE   PALEO-FRIENDLY

SERVES 4

PREP TIME: 10 MINUTES • COOK TIME: 30 MINUTES TO 1 HOUR ON HIGH

Garlicky chimichurri sauce is a staple in Argentina and is typically served with steak. But the flavors are a surprisingly bright, flavorful complement to fish.

FOR THE COD

½ cup chicken broth

½ cup dry white wine

Zest and juice of 1 lemon

4 (4-ounce) cod fillets

Sea salt

Freshly ground black pepper

FOR THE CHIMICHURRI

1 cup chopped fresh parsley leaves

¼ cup chopped fresh cilantro leaves

½ cup olive oil

¼ cup white wine vinegar

2 garlic cloves

1. In the slow cooker, mix the broth, wine, and lemon zest and juice. Add the cod and season generously with salt and pepper.

2. Cover and cook on High for 30 minutes to 1 hour (depending on the thickness of the fillets), or until the fish flakes easily with a fork.

3. Meanwhile, make the chimichurri: In a blender, mix the parsley, cilantro, oil, vinegar, and garlic, and pulse until smooth. Season with salt and pepper.

4. Serve the poached cod with a spoonful of chimichurri sauce.

Variation: Use whatever fish is available and in season, but adjust the cooking time depending on the thickness of the fish. Thinner fillets, such as rock fish or tilapia, cook in less time than those that are 1 inch or thicker.

Nutritional Information per Serving: Calories: 356; Fat: 26g; Protein: 18g; Carbohydrates: 3g; Sugar: 1g; Sodium: 475mg

Tilapia Piccata with Spinach

GLUTEN-FREE **PALEO-FRIENDLY**

SERVES 4

PREP TIME: 5 MINUTES • COOK TIME: 30 MINUTES TO 1 HOUR ON HIGH

Tilapia and spinach both cook quickly and do well with a quick steam or poach, making the slow cooker a perfect vessel to cook both at the same time.

1 tablespoon butter

8 cups spinach, roughly chopped

¼ cup vermouth or dry white wine

¼ cup capers, drained

1 teaspoon minced garlic

4 (5-ounce) tilapia fillets

Sea salt

Freshly ground black pepper

1. Butter the inside of the slow cooker crock.

2. In the slow cooker, mix the spinach, vermouth, capers, and garlic. Top with the tilapia. Season with salt and pepper.

3. Cover and cook on High for 30 minutes to 1 hour, or until the fish flakes easily with a fork.

Nutritional Highlight: One cup of cooked spinach contains nearly 1,000 percent of your daily value of vitamin K. It's also rich in vitamins A, E, and C; folate; magnesium; iron; copper; B vitamins; calcium; potassium; and zinc.

Nutritional Information per Serving: Calories: 169, Fat: 5g; Protein: 28g; Carbohydrates: 3g; Sugar: 0g; Sodium: 432mg

Lobster Risotto

SERVES 4

PREP TIME: 10 MINUTES • COOK TIME: 2 HOURS ON HIGH

Risotto is delicious, but sometimes you just don't feel like all the stirring required to make it. Let the slow cooker do the work for you! To make this a complete meal, serve with a side salad.

1 tablespoon butter

1 pound cooked lobster meat

4 cups chicken broth

½ cup dry white wine

1 cup short-grain or Arborio rice

1 onion, diced

1 tablespoon minced fresh tarragon leaves, plus more for serving

1 tablespoon olive oil

Sea salt

Freshly ground black pepper

1. Butter the inside of the slow cooker crock.

2. In the slow cooker, mix the lobster, broth, wine, rice, onion, tarragon, and oil. Season with salt and pepper.

3. Cover and cook on High for 2 hours. Garnish with fresh tarragon.

Variation: If lobster is difficult to find or too expensive, use crab claw meat instead and swap the tarragon for fresh chives or marjoram.

Nutritional Information per Serving: Calories: 404, Fat: 9g; Protein: 30g; Carbohydrates: 42g; Sugar: 2g; Sodium: 1,398mg

Pork and Poultry

Roasted Tomatillo Chicken Soup

GLUTEN-FREE **PALEO-FRIENDLY**

SERVES 4

PREP TIME: 10 MINUTES • COOK TIME: 2 HOURS ON LOW

Tomatillos bring a surprising tangy flavor to this chicken soup. This recipe uses precooked chicken to save time. If you prefer, you can use raw chicken instead. Just increase the cooking time by 1 hour if using diced raw chicken breasts or 2 hours if using whole chicken breasts that you plan to cut into pieces after cooking.

4 cups chicken broth, divided

1 cup roughly chopped fresh cilantro
    leaves, divided

4 cups tomatillos

1 cup finely chopped onion

4 garlic cloves

Pinch red pepper flakes

Sea salt

2 cups cubed cooked chicken

Juice of 1 lime

1 avocado, sliced

1. In a blender, mix ½ cup of the chicken broth, ½ cup of the cilantro, the tomatillos, onion, garlic, and red pepper, and purée until smooth. Season with salt. In the slow cooker, mix the broth mixture and the remaining 3½ cups of chicken broth. Add the chicken.

2. Cover and cook on Low for 2 hours.

3. Just before serving, stir in the lime juice.

4. Garnish with the avocado and the remaining ½ cup of cilantro.

Nutritional Highlight: Tomatillos are a member of the nightshade family, which includes tomatoes, eggplants, potatoes, and sweet and hot peppers. Tomatillos are an excellent source of dietary fiber, vitamins C and K, niacin, potassium, and manganese.

Nutritional Information per Serving: Calories: 326; Fat: 15g; Protein: 32g; Carbohydrates: 17g; Sugar: 3g; Sodium: 919mg

Herb-Roasted Chicken

GLUTEN-FREE **PALEO-FRIENDLY**

SERVES 4 TO 6

PREP TIME: 10 MINUTES • COOK TIME: 4 TO 6 HOURS ON HIGH

While you could make roast chicken in the oven, your slow cooker provides a naturally moist environment to keep the bird succulent and tender. Unlike cooking in the oven, you needn't baste it.

¼ cup olive oil

½ cup finely chopped fresh
parsley leaves

2 tablespoons fresh thyme leaves

1 fresh rosemary sprig, leaves only

Sea salt

Freshly ground black pepper

1 onion, cut into rings

1 (3- to 4-pound) whole chicken, giblets
removed

1. In a mini food processor fitted with the metal blade or using a mortar and pestle, blend the oil, parsley, thyme, and rosemary to a thick paste. Season with salt and pepper.

2. In the slow cooker, arrange the onion rings in a single layer.

3. Season the inside of the chicken with salt and pepper. Using your hands, thoroughly coat the chicken with the prepared herb paste, gently lifting the skin to rub some underneath as well. Put the chicken on top of the onions.

4. Cover and cook on High for 4 to 6 hours, or until the chicken reaches 165°F in the thickest part of the thigh when tested with a meat thermometer.

Tip: Don't throw away the leftover chicken bones! Make chicken broth. Simply add the chicken carcass to a clean slow cooker along with some chopped onion, carrots, and celery, and season with salt. Cover with cold water. Simmer for 6 to 8 hours on Low. Set aside to cool, then strain and store in an airtight container in the refrigerator for up to 3 days.

Nutritional Information per Serving: Calories: 738; Fat: 55g; Protein: 61g; Carbohydrates: 4g; Sugar: 1g; Sodium: 337mg

Chicken Saltimbocca

SERVES 4

PREP TIME: 10 MINUTES • COOK TIME: 2 HOURS ON HIGH OR 4 HOURS ON LOW

Saltimbocca means "jump in your mouth" in Italian and is traditionally a panfried dish made with veal. This version uses chicken and a delicious combination of spinach and Parmesan, wrapped in prosciutto. Enjoy with a side salad and roasted potatoes.

4 (5-ounce) skinless boneless
   chicken breasts

4 slices prosciutto

1 cup frozen spinach, thawed and
   squeezed of excess moisture

¼ cup freshly grated Parmesan cheese

½ cup white wine

½ cup chicken broth

1. Put the chicken breasts between two pieces of parchment paper and, using a mallet, pound the chicken to about ⅓ of an inch thick.

2. Remove the top sheet of parchment and lay one slice of prosciutto on top of each chicken breast. Top each piece of chicken with one-quarter of the spinach and one-quarter of the Parmesan. Using your fingers, gently roll up each piece of chicken and secure with a toothpick.

3. In the slow cooker, place the chicken rolls and pour in the wine and broth.

4. Cover and cook on Low for 4 hours or on High for 2 hours.

Nutritional Highlight: You might not think of prosciutto as healthy, but it provides a lot of flavor for surprisingly few calories. In fact, just one thin slice of prosciutto has only 30 calories and 4 grams of protein. Given that prosciutto already contributes sodium to the dish, no additional salt is used.

Nutritional Information per Serving: Calories: 354, Fat: 13g; Protein: 49g; Carbohydrates: 2g; Sugar: 0g; Sodium: 546mg

Chicken Cassoulet

GLUTEN-FREE

SERVES 4 TO 6

PREP TIME: 10 MINUTES • COOK TIME: 6 TO 8 HOURS ON LOW

The word cassoulet *makes this chicken dish sound fussy, but it's actually very easy to put together and very healthy! Beans, celery, carrots, and onions provide satisfying fiber and important vitamins and minerals. Chicken thighs are rich in protein. A small amount of pork sausage adds rich flavor to the dish.*

2 cups chicken broth

2 (15-ounce) cans great Northern beans,
    rinsed and drained

6 to 8 bone-in chicken thighs,
    skin removed

1 pork sausage, cut into ½-inch pieces

1 cup white wine

1 cup canned diced tomatoes, with juice

1 cup diced carrots

1 cup diced celery

1 cup diced onions

4 to 6 garlic cloves, smashed

Sea salt

Freshly ground black pepper

1. In the slow cooker, mix the broth, beans, chicken, sausage, wine, tomatoes, carrots, celery, onions, and garlic. Season with salt and pepper.

2. Cover and cook on Low for 6 to 8 hours.

3. To serve, transfer the chicken pieces to a serving platter or individual plates, and place the beans, pork, and vegetables alongside.

Tip: Using bone-in chicken keeps the meat moist through the long cooking process. However, if you prefer the convenience of boneless chicken thighs, reduce the total cooking time to 4 to 5 hours.

Nutritional Information per Serving: Calories: 472, Fat: 12g; Protein: 34g; Carbohydrates: 46g; Sugar: 7g; Sodium: 653mg

Chicken Curry

GLUTEN-FREE **PALEO-FRIENDLY**

SERVES 6 TO 8

PREP TIME: 5 MINUTES • COOK TIME: 4 HOURS ON LOW

This spicy yellow curry is naturally low in carbohydrates, making it an excellent choice if you're observing a low-carb or paleo-style diet.

2 pounds boneless chicken thighs, diced

2 (15-ounce) cans diced fire-roasted tomatoes, with juice

1 large onion, diced

1 tablespoon curry powder

1 teaspoon garam masala

Sea salt

Freshly ground black pepper

Steamed brown rice, for serving (optional)

Lemon wedges, for serving

1. In the slow cooker, mix the chicken, tomatoes, onion, curry powder, and garam masala. Season with salt and pepper.

2. Cover and cook on Low for 4 hours.

3. Serve over steamed rice (if using) and garnish with lemon wedges.

Tip: To make your own yellow curry powder, mix 2 tablespoons turmeric, 1 tablespoon each ground coriander and ground cumin, 1 teaspoon each ground cinnamon and ground ginger, and ½ teaspoon each dry mustard, ground cardamom, and cayenne.

Nutritional Information per Serving: Calories: 235; Fat: 8g; Protein: 30g; Carbohydrates: 9g; Sugar: 5g; Sodium: 354mg

Chicken Cacciatore

GLUTEN-FREE **PALEO-FRIENDLY**

SERVES 4 TO 6

PREP TIME: 5 MINUTES • COOK TIME: 6 HOURS ON LOW

Cacciatore is a traditional Italian preparation for meats and loosely translates to "in the hunter style." The type of wine, white or red, used to help tenderize the meat and create a flavorful sauce varies by region. We use red wine in this recipe, but you can use whatever you prefer.

1 cup dry red wine

1 cup chicken broth

1 (28-ounce) can plum tomatoes, with juice

1 red pepper, sliced

1 onion, sliced

1 cup sliced mushrooms

4 garlic cloves, smashed

Sea salt

Freshly ground black pepper

6 to 8 bone-in chicken thighs, skin removed

1. In the slow cooker, mix the wine, broth, tomatoes, red pepper, onion, mushrooms, and garlic. Season with salt and pepper.

2. Put the chicken pieces on top of the vegetable mixture.

3. Cover and cook on Low for 6 hours.

Nutritional Highlight: Broth made from chicken bones is surprisingly rich in minerals, particularly calcium, magnesium, and phosphorus. It also contains nutrients from the broken-down cartilage and tendons that may support bone and joint health.

Nutritional Information per Serving: Calories: 360; Fat: 10g; Protein: 39g; Carbohydrates: 18g; Sugar: 11g; Sodium: 281mg

Chicken Fricassee

GLUTEN-FREE **PALEO-FRIENDLY**

SERVES 6 TO 8

PREP TIME: 10 MINUTES • COOK TIME: 6 HOURS ON LOW

A fricassee is a traditional French stew that lends itself perfectly to the slow cooker. This dish is incredibly versatile—you can use whatever meat and vegetables you have on hand. Combine flavors that you enjoy with ingredients that are in season or on sale.

2 pounds boneless chicken thighs,
   cut into 1-inch pieces

2 cups chicken broth

½ cup white wine

2 cups sliced mushrooms

1 fennel bulb, cored and thinly sliced

1 onion, diced

4 garlic cloves, smashed

¼ cup chopped fresh parsley leaves

Sea salt

Freshly ground black pepper

1. In the slow cooker, mix the chicken, broth, wine, mushrooms, fennel, onion, garlic, and parsley. Season with salt and pepper.

2. Cover and cook on Low for 6 hours.

Nutritional Highlight: Chicken thighs tend to retain more moisture when cooked than chicken breasts. While thighs do contain about 30 more calories per 3-ounce serving, they also contain more iron and zinc. Just be sure to remove the skin to slash the amount of fat.

Nutritional Information per Serving: Calories: 373; Fat: 12g; Protein: 48g; Carbohydrates: 11g; Sugar: 2g; Sodium: 477mg

Turkey Vegetable Soup

GLUTEN-FREE

SERVES 4 TO 6

PREP TIME: 10 MINUTES • COOK TIME: 4 HOURS ON LOW

This recipe is a great way to use up leftover turkey or chicken meat when you have roasted the whole bird and are looking to spruce up the leftovers. Use quinoa pasta if you want to keep the dish gluten-free.

4 cups cooked turkey, light and
   dark meat

4 cups chicken broth

4 cups vegetable broth

2 cups diced green beans

4 carrots, diced

2 celery stalks, diced

1 onion, thinly sliced

1 tablespoon minced garlic

1 tablespoon dried Italian herb blend

Sea salt

Freshly ground black pepper

1 cup frozen peas, thawed

8 ounces dried whole wheat pasta shells

1. In the slow cooker, mix the turkey, broths, beans, carrots, celery, onion, garlic, and herbs. Season with salt and pepper.

2. Cover and cook on Low for 4 hours.

3. In the final 30 minutes of cooking, stir in the peas and pasta. Cover and cook until the pasta is tender.

Tip: When you're cooking for long periods of time, as is the case with slow cooking, using dried herbs generally works better. Fresh herbs tend to lose their bright flavors when cooked unless added at the very end of the cooking process. (For more information, see page 18 in "Slow Cooker Basics.")

Nutritional Information per Serving: Calories: 602; Fat: 11g; Protein: 63g; Carbohydrates: 64g; Sugar: 8g; Sodium: 1,769mg

Cranberry Turkey Roast

GLUTEN-FREE **PALEO-FRIENDLY**

SERVES 6 TO 8

PREP TIME: 10 MINUTES • COOK TIME: 8 HOURS ON LOW

If you consider the best parts of Thanksgiving dinner the turkey and cranberry sauce, this recipe is for you. But don't wait until November to enjoy it: Turkey is an excellent source of protein and selenium, a critical nutrient for the production of active thyroid hormone.

1 (3-pound) turkey breast

Sea salt

Freshly ground black pepper

1 (16-ounce) bag fresh cranberries

1 cup apple cider

Zest and juice of 1 orange

1 fresh rosemary sprig

1. Season the turkey breast with salt and pepper.

2. In the slow cooker, mix the cranberries, apple cider, orange zest and juice, and rosemary. Place the turkey into this mixture.

3. Cover and cook on Low for 8 hours.

Tip: If you are making this out of season and cannot find fresh or frozen cranberries, you may substitute cranberry sauce, but pay attention to the sugar content—many cranberry sauces are sweeter than jam or honey.

Nutritional Information per Serving: Calories: 305; Fat: 4g; Protein: 39g; Carbohydrates: 27g; Sugar: 18g; Sodium: 2,344mg

Duck à l'Orange

SERVES 4

PREP TIME: 10 MINUTES • COOK TIME: 1 TO 2 HOURS ON LOW

Although the slow cooker isn't a particularly French method for cooking duck, it does provide the gentle heat needed to yield a succulent, flavorful piece of meat. To keep the crispiness in the skin, refrain from pouring the orange juice and broth over it; instead pour it around the duck breasts.

4 (5-ounce) duck breasts

Sea salt

Freshly ground black pepper

1 cup orange juice

½ cup chicken broth

2 tablespoons orange liqueur, such as Grand Marnier

1 teaspoon cornstarch

1. Using a sharp knife, score the duck breasts by cutting through the outer layer of skin in a diamond-like pattern. Be careful not to cut all the way through the fat. Season with salt and pepper.

2. In a large skillet over medium heat, cook the duck skin-side down for about 5 minutes. (It should render a significant amount of fat.) Remove the pan from the heat. Spoon about 1 tablespoon of the rendered fat into the slow cooker to thoroughly coat the crock. Reserve the remaining fat for another purpose.

3. In the slow cooker, put the duck breasts skin-side up.

4. In a small measuring cup, whisk together the orange juice, broth, liqueur, and cornstarch. Pour this mixture around the duck.

5. Cover and cook on Low for 1 to 2 hours, or until the duck registers 145°F on a meat thermometer.

Nutritional Highlight: While duck skin contains a thick layer of fat, the meat beneath is actually quite lean—more so than either chicken or turkey—and is a good source of iron, selenium, zinc, and B vitamins.

Nutritional Information per Serving: Calories: 258; Fat: 6g; Protein: 32g; Carbohydrates: 7g; Sugar: 5g; Sodium: 154mg

Thai Red Curry with Duck and Pineapple

GLUTEN-FREE **PALEO-FRIENDLY**

SERVES 4

PREP TIME: 10 MINUTES • COOK TIME: 2 TO 3 HOURS ON LOW

The unique flavors of this Thai curry dish are sure to make it a family favorite. It offers the perfect balance of flavors—sweet, sour, salty, and savory. Serve it with steamed brown jasmine rice to provide the perfect balance of nutrients.

2 (15-ounce) cans coconut milk

¼ cup red curry paste

5 Kaffir lime leaves

2 fresh Thai basil sprigs (optional)

1 green pepper, sliced

1 plum tomato, diced

1 small onion, thinly sliced

16 ounces Chinese-roasted duck, cut into 2-inch pieces

1 (15-ounce) can unsweetened pineapple chunks, drained

1 tablespoon fish sauce

1. In the slow cooker, mix the coconut milk, curry paste, lime leaves, basil (if using), green pepper, tomato, and onion. Add the duck and stir to coat well.

2. Cover and cook on Low for 2 to 3 hours.

3. Just before serving, stir in the pineapple and fish sauce.

Tip: Thai basil can be found in Asian markets, where it is generally less expensive than the Mediterranean version. Thai basil also holds up better during cooking and has a slightly more pronounced anise flavor.

Nutritional Information per Serving: Calories: 869; Fat: 69g; Protein: 33g; Carbohydrates: 37g; Sugar: 20g; Sodium: 1,323mg

Smoky Pork Taco Filling

GLUTEN-FREE **PALEO-FRIENDLY**

SERVES 6 TO 8

PREP TIME: 5 MINUTES • COOK TIME: 8 TO 10 HOURS ON LOW

Smoked paprika and sherry vinegar elevate this basic taco filling to something extraordinary. Enjoy it on small (4-inch) corn tortillas for a traditional Mexico City-inspired feast.

1 tablespoon olive oil

1 pound boneless pork loin

1 cup canned tomato sauce or Basic Marinara Sauce (page 186)

¼ cup sherry vinegar or red wine vinegar

1 cup diced onion

1 tablespoon roasted garlic

1 tablespoon smoked paprika

1 teaspoon ground cumin

1. Coat the bottom of the slow cooker crock with the oil. In the slow cooker, place the pork loin.

2. In a small mixing bowl, whisk together the tomato sauce, vinegar, onion, garlic, paprika, and cumin. Pour over the pork loin.

3. Cover and cook on Low for 8 to 10 hours.

4. Let the meat rest for 10 to 15 minutes. Transfer to a cutting board and, using a sharp knife, slice the meat and then finely chop.

Tip: Whisk the sauce ingredients together and prepare all the additional taco fillings the night before, so when you wake up you can put the pork loin into the slow cooker, head to work or out for a day of play, and arrive at home to a fully prepared meal.

Nutritional Information per Serving: Calories: 155; Fat: 5g; Protein: 21g; Carbohydrates: 5g; Sugar: 3g; Sodium: 259mg

Bánh Mì Filling

PALEO-FRIENDLY

SERVES 6 TO 8

PREP TIME: 5 MINUTES • COOK TIME: 4 TO 6 HOURS ON LOW

Bánh Mì, pronounced "bon-me," is a traditional Vietnamese sandwich that has become the darling of foodies. Classic preparations of this sandwich include sour carrots and daikon radish, fresh cilantro, cucumber, and spicy mayonnaise.

2 pounds boneless pork loin,
   thinly sliced

½ cup chicken broth

1 onion, finely chopped

¼ cup roast pork seasoning mix,
   found in Asian markets

Sea salt

Freshly ground black pepper

1. In the slow cooker, mix the pork, broth, onion, and pork seasoning. Season with salt and pepper.

2. Cover and cook on Low for 4 to 6 hours.

Tip: To make the pickled-carrot-and-daikon-radish slaw that's ubiquitous on Bánh Mì sandwiches, mix ½ cup each julienned carrots and daikon radish with ½ cup white vinegar, ½ cup water, and 2 tablespoons granulated sugar in an airtight jar. Shake to combine and season with salt. Cover and refrigerate for at least 30 minutes, but not longer than overnight. (It becomes wilted and tasteless if left too long.)

Nutritional Information per Serving: Calories: 244; Fat: 5g; Protein: 40g; Carbohydrates: 6g; Sugar: 2g; Sodium: 635mg

Texas–Style Pulled Pork

SERVES 8 TO 10

PREP TIME: 5 MINUTES • COOK TIME: 6 TO 8 HOURS ON LOW

Everything's bigger in Texas, including the flavors. Unfortunately, so, too, is the sugar content in traditional pulled pork. Instead of slathering the pork shoulder with a sweet, highly processed barbecue sauce, allow the natural flavors of onion, garlic, and spices to permeate the dish while it cooks in your slow cooker. If desired, serve a small amount of prepared barbecue sauce on the side.

1 to 2 tablespoons oil

3 to 4 pounds boneless pork shoulder

Sea salt

Freshly ground black pepper

1 cup chicken broth

½ cup apple cider vinegar

1 large onion, finely diced

2 tablespoons tomato paste

1 tablespoon minced garlic

2 teaspoons ground cumin

2 teaspoons smoked paprika

1 teaspoon ground coriander

1 teaspoon dry mustard

1 tablespoon coconut palm sugar

8 whole-grain hamburger buns,
    for serving

1. Grease the bottom of the slow cooker crock with the oil.

2. Season the pork with salt and pepper and put it in the slow cooker.

3. In a small bowl, whisk together the broth, vinegar, onion, tomato paste, garlic, cumin, paprika, coriander, and dry mustard. Pour over the pork.

4. Cover and cook on Low for 6 to 8 hours, or until the meat can be easily shredded with a fork.

5. Using two forks, gently shred the pork into pieces. Add the sugar and stir to combine well. Serve on hamburger buns.

Variation: To reduce carbs in this dish, serve this dish as an open-face sandwich on half of a hamburger bun or skip the bun altogether and serve over shredded red cabbage.

Nutritional Information per Serving: Calories: 410; Fat: 10g; Protein: 52g; Carbohydrates: 28g; Sugar: 6g; Sodium: 432mg

Pork Ribs

GLUTEN-FREE

SERVES 4 TO 6

PREP TIME: 5 MINUTES • COOK TIME: 8 TO 10 HOURS ON LOW

Pork ribs probably aren't the first food you think of when you hear the word healthy, *but you can enjoy them occasionally if they are prepared with whole ingredients. This slow cooker version makes it easy to do so.*

1 onion, thinly sliced

2 pounds pork ribs

Sea salt

Freshly ground black pepper

1 cup chicken broth

1 cup tomato ketchup

¼ cup apple cider vinegar

4 garlic cloves, smashed

1 tablespoon ground cumin

1 tablespoon smoked paprika

1. In the slow cooker, layer the onion slices on the bottom and top with the pork ribs. Season generously with salt and pepper.

2. In a measuring cup, whisk together the broth, ketchup, vinegar, garlic, cumin, and paprika. Pour over the pork ribs.

3. Cover and cook on Low for 8 to 10 hours.

Variation: If you prefer to use boneless pork ribs, reduce the cooking time by 2 hours.

Nutritional Information per Serving: Calories: 717; Fat: 41g; Protein: 63g; Carbohydrates: 21g; Sugar: 15g; Sodium: 1,054mg

Pork Adovada

GLUTEN-FREE **PALEO-FRIENDLY**

SERVES 4 TO 6

PREP TIME: 10 MINUTES • COOK TIME: 4 TO 6 HOURS ON LOW

New Mexico's take on the Spanish recipe for marinated pork, or adobada, is a perfect filling for tacos, burritos, or enchiladas. Because it is prepared in a slow cooker, this adovada requires no added oil.

2 to 3 pounds pork loin, cubed

1 small onion, diced

4 to 6 garlic cloves, smashed

2 chiles in adobo sauce, minced,
   plus 1 tablespoon sauce

½ cup apple cider vinegar

1 cup Basic Marinara Sauce (page 186)

1 tablespoon ground cumin

1 teaspoon smoked paprika

1. In the slow cooker, mix the pork, onion, garlic, and chiles.

2. In a small mixing bowl, whisk together the adobo sauce, cider vinegar, marinara sauce, cumin, and paprika. Pour over the pork and onion mixture.

3. Cover and cook on Low for 4 to 6 hours.

Variation: To make a savory soup, add 4 cups of chicken broth in step 2. To serve, garnish with avocado and fresh cilantro.

Nutritional Information per Serving: Calories: 694; Fat: 35g; Protein: 71g; Carbohydrates: 19g; Sugar: 8g; Sodium: 755mg

Ginger Pork with Baby Bok Choy

GLUTEN-FREE **PALEO-FRIENDLY**

SERVES 4

PREP TIME: 10 MINUTES • COOK TIME: 6 TO 8 HOURS ON LOW

Bok choy is a common ingredient in traditional Chinese medicine, but Westerners are finding many reasons to love this leafy green. It is rich in vitamins A, B₆, C, and K and manganese, iron, calcium, and magnesium—and it's delicious in this pork dish. (Be sure to thoroughly rinse the bok choy to remove any residual dirt or sediment.)

2 tablespoons toasted sesame oil

1 onion, thinly sliced into rings

4 boneless pork chops

Sea salt

Freshly ground black pepper

½ cup chicken broth

¼ cup soy sauce

2 tablespoons rice wine vinegar

1 tablespoon minced fresh ginger

4 baby bok choy, halved lengthwise

1. In the slow cooker, mix the sesame oil and onion.

2. Season the pork chops lightly with salt and pepper, and put them on top of the onion.

3. In a small bowl, whisk together the broth, soy sauce, vinegar, and ginger. Pour over the pork chops.

4. Lay the bok choy cut-side down over the pork chops.

5. Cover and cook on Low for 6 to 8 hours.

Tip: If you don't have toasted sesame oil in your pantry, consider picking up this Asian cooking staple. It works in a variety of dishes, from salad dressings to marinades, and has a naturally high smoke point.

Nutritional Information per Serving: Calories: 307; Fat: 12g; Protein: 40g; Carbohydrates: 6g; Sugar: 2g; Sodium: 1,179mg

Peppery Pork in Port Sauce

GLUTEN-FREE **PALEO-FRIENDLY**

SERVES 4

PREP TIME: 10 MINUTES • COOK TIME: 8 HOURS ON LOW

The flavors of onion, apple, spicy black pepper, and sweet port wine combine in a luxurious sauce to complement perfectly cooked pork tenderloin.

1 small onion, cut into thick rings

2 apples, cored and cut into thick wedges

1 to 2 pounds boneless pork tenderloin

½ teaspoon sea salt

1 tablespoon freshly ground black pepper

½ cup beef broth

¼ cup port wine

1. In the slow cooker, arrange the apples and onion in the bottom.

2. Season the pork tenderloin with salt and pepper. Put on top of the apples and onions. Add the beef broth and port.

3. Cover and cook on Low for 8 hours.

Tip: You could spend a small fortune on a good bottle of port, but for cooking purposes, an inexpensive bottle of ruby port will work well.

Nutritional Information per Serving: Calories: 225; Fat: 6g; Protein: 25g; Carbohydrates: 16g; Sugar: 10g; Sodium: 389mg

Pork with Caramelized Onions and Chard

GLUTEN-FREE **PALEO-FRIENDLY**

SERVES 6 TO 8

PREP TIME: 10 MINUTES • COOK TIME: 6 TO 8 HOURS ON LOW

Technique is everything when it comes to healthy cooking. When prepared properly, natural ingredients can bring so much flavor to a dish, reducing the amount of sugar, fat, or salt needed. Onions are a perfect example: long, slow cooking brings out their natural sugars and adds a rich, sweet yet savory flavor to dishes.

1 tablespoon butter

2 onions, sliced in thin rings

1 tablespoon olive oil

Sea salt

Pinch sugar

Freshly ground black pepper

2 to 3 pounds boneless pork loin

1 cup chicken broth

1 bunch chard, roughly chopped

1. Butter the bottom of the slow cooker crock.

2. In the slow cooker, mix the onions and oil. Season with salt and a small pinch of sugar.

3. Season the pork loin with salt and pepper. Put on top of the onions. Pour in the broth.

4. Cover and cook on Low for 6 to 8 hours.

5. In the final 30 minutes of cooking, put the chard on top of the other ingredients and cook until tender.

Nutritional Highlight: Swiss chard contains a whopping 13 different polyphenol antioxidants. Be careful, though: The antioxidant content of most plants decreases with cooking, particularly the long cooking times involved in slow cooking. So, add them in the last 30 minutes of cooking to preserve their nutritional value.

Nutritional Information per Serving: Calories: 277; Fat: 10g; Protein: 41g; Carbohydrates: 4g; Sugar: 2g; Sodium: 279mg

Pork Chops with Figs and Shallots

GLUTEN-FREE **PALEO-FRIENDLY**

SERVES 4

PREP TIME: 5 MINUTES • COOK TIME: 8 HOURS ON LOW

Figs are a classic pairing for pork. Here, fresh whole figs are combined with fig butter for the ultimate effect.

1 cup roughly chopped fresh figs

2 shallots, roughly chopped

½ cup white wine

4 bone-in pork chops

Sea salt

Freshly ground black pepper

½ cup fig butter or jam

1. In the slow cooker, mix the figs, shallots, and wine.

2. Season the pork chops with salt and pepper, and then spread them with the fig butter. Put the prepared pork chops on top of the fig and shallot mixture.

3. Cover and cook on Low for 8 hours.

Nutritional Highlight: Figs contain a generous amount of fiber and are also rich in vitamin B_6, copper, potassium, manganese, and pantothenic acid. Potassium is a critical nutrient often in short supply in modern diets. It helps regulate blood pressure and muscle contraction.

Nutritional Information per Serving: Calories: 425; Fat: 20g; Protein: 19g; Carbohydrates: 36g; Sugar: 22g; Sodium: 129mg

9

Beef and Lamb

■ ■

Beef Stew

GLUTEN-FREE **PALEO-FRIENDLY**

SERVES 4 TO 6

PREP TIME: 15 MINUTES • COOK TIME: 8 HOURS ON LOW

For those mornings when you only have a few minutes to prepare dinner on your way out the door, this beef stew comes to the rescue. Simply throw all the ingredients in the slow cooker, cover, and let it simmer all day long.

1 cup diced carrots

1 cup diced onions

1 cup diced celery

1 pound beef chuck, cut into 1-inch pieces

4 cups fingerling potatoes

1 cup white wine

2 cups beef broth or water

1 bay leaf

Sea salt

Freshly ground black pepper

1 to 2 tablespoons cold butter (optional)

1. Layer the ingredients in the slow cooker in the following order: carrots, onion, celery, beef, and potatoes. Pour the wine and broth over them. Add the bay leaf. Season generously with salt and pepper.

2. Cover and cook on Low for 8 hours.

3. To serve, transfer the beef and potatoes to a serving platter. Discard the bay leaf.

4. Using a stand or immersion blender, purée the remaining vegetables and cooking liquid with the butter (if using) until smooth. Return the beef and potatoes to the slow cooker and stir to combine.

Tip: To save time, purchase diced carrots, onions, and celery in the prepared foods section of the produce department.

Nutritional Information per Serving: Calories: 437; Fat: 11g; Protein: 40g; Carbohydrates: 32g; Sugar: 5g; Sodium: 590mg

Beer-Braised Beef

SERVES 4 TO 6

PREP TIME: 10 MINUTES • COOK TIME: 8 HOURS ON LOW

While the French are famous for cooking meat in wine, Americans have perfected cooking with beer. Although it may not enjoy the same high-brow reputation, this beef stew is just as tender and flavorful.

2 cups sliced onion

2 garlic cloves, crushed

2 pounds beef chuck, cut into
   1-inch pieces

¼ cup all-purpose flour

20 ounces dark beer, such as stout
   or porter

4 cups beef broth

2 fresh thyme sprigs

1. In the slow cooker, mix the onions and garlic.

2. Dredge the beef in the flour and put on top of the onions and garlic. Pour in the beer and beef broth. Add the thyme.

3. Cover and cook on Low for 8 hours.

Variation: For even more flavor, brown the beef on the stove top before putting it in the slow cooker: Pat it dry with paper towels, then dredge in the flour. In a medium skillet over medium-high heat, heat 2 tablespoons of oil and cook beef until browned on all sides. Stir in about 1 cup of the beer, scraping up any browned bits that have collected on the bottom of the pan. Transfer mixture to the slow cooker, add the thyme, and cook as directed.

Nutritional Information per Serving: Calories: 806; Fat: 29g; Protein: 114g; Carbohydrates: 13g; Sugar: 3g; Sodium: 1,011mg

Beef Steak au Poivre

GLUTEN-FREE **PALEO-FRIENDLY**

SERVES 4

PREP TIME: 10 MINUTES • COOK TIME: 3 HOURS ON HIGH OR 8 HOURS ON LOW

Pan-searing the beef ahead of time will improve the flavors of this classic French dish, but if you're short on time, you can skip this step and put all the ingredients in the slow cooker together. The classic preparation of this dish uses heavy cream to thicken the sauce. This version lightens things up by puréeing the cooking liquid to create the delicious sauce.

1½ pounds beef steak

1 tablespoon freshly ground black pepper

½ teaspoon sea salt

2 tablespoons olive oil

¼ cup minced shallots

1 garlic clove, smashed

1 cup dry red wine

4 cups beef broth

1. Pat the steak pieces dry with a paper towel. Season with salt and pepper.

2. In a medium skillet over medium-high heat, heat the oil. Sear prepared beef until browned on all sides. (You may have to do this in batches so as not to crowd the pan.)

3. Transfer the browned pieces of meat to the slow cooker. Top with the shallots and garlic. Pour in the wine and broth.

4. Cover and cook on High for 3 hours or on Low for 8 hours.

5. Transfer the meat to a serving platter. Using a stand or immersion blender, purée the cooking liquid until smooth. Pour the sauce over the meat and serve.

Variation: If you prefer a richer sauce, transfer the cooking liquid and vegetables to a small saucepan and reduce by half. Remove from the heat and purée.

Nutritional Information per Serving: Calories: 476; Fat: 19g; Protein: 57g; Carbohydrates: 6g; Sugar: 1g; Sodium: 1,114mg

Braised Beef with Currants, Parsley, and Pine Nuts

GLUTEN-FREE **PALEO-FRIENDLY**

SERVES 4

PREP TIME: 5 MINUTES • COOK TIME: 8 HOURS ON LOW

Beef, currants, and pine nuts are a surprisingly pleasing combination in this rustic, Mediterranean-inspired braised dish. The natural sweetness of the currants makes it especially appealing to children.

1 tablespoon olive oil

1½ pounds beef chuck, cut into
    1-inch pieces

1 onion, cut into rings

½ cup dried currants

1 teaspoon finely grated lemon zest

¼ teaspoon ground cinnamon

1 cup red wine

1 cup beef broth

Sea salt

Freshly ground black pepper

½ cup roughly chopped fresh
    parsley leaves

½ cup toasted pine nuts (optional)

1. Grease the inside of the slow cooker crock with the oil.

2. In the slow cooker, mix the beef and onion. Add the currants, lemon zest, and cinnamon. Pour in the wine and broth. Season with salt and pepper.

3. Cover and cook on Low for 8 hours.

4. To serve, garnish with the parsley and pine nuts (if using).

Tip: To toast pine nuts, heat a dry skillet over medium-low heat. Cook the pine nuts, stirring occasionally, for 2 to 3 minutes, until golden brown and fragrant.

Nutritional Information per Serving: Calories: 542; Fat: 26g; Protein: 56g; Carbohydrates: 9g; Sugar: 4g; Sodium: 396mg

Corned Beef and Cabbage

GLUTEN-FREE **PALEO-FRIENDLY**

SERVES 4

PREP TIME: 5 MINUTES • COOK TIME: 4 HOURS ON LOW

Don't wait until St. Patrick's Day to enjoy this hearty meal. While corned beef might not be considered as healthy as other cuts of meat, it is usually made with brisket, which meets the guidelines for the designation of "lean," according to a 2005 USDA report. If you're concerned about fat intake, discard the fat from the slow cooker before serving.

1 large head cabbage, cored and sliced

1 small onion, finely chopped

4 cups chicken broth

1 pound cooked corned beef, thinly sliced

Sea salt

Freshly ground black pepper

1. In the slow cooker, mix the cabbage and onion. Pour the broth over the vegetables. Add the beef. Season with salt and pepper.

2. Cover and cook on Low for 4 hours.

Nutritional Highlight: Cabbage contains potent anticancer compounds. To retain the most nutrients, enjoy it raw or cooked over low heat, as in this recipe.

Nutritional Information per Serving: Calories: 409; Fat: 23g; Protein: 30g; Carbohydrates: 21g; Sugar: 11g; Sodium: 2,164mg

Steak Carnitas

GLUTEN-FREE PALEO-FRIENDLY

SERVES 4 TO 6

PREP TIME: 10 MINUTES • COOK TIME: 6 TO 8 HOURS ON LOW

Pork simmered in broth and seasonings is the perfect filling for tacos or enchiladas, especially when you're entertaining guests and need an easy, fun, filling meal. Bonus: The meat is cooked in its own juices and a bit of citrus juice, which means more flavor and fewer calories.

1½ pounds beef chuck, cut into
    1-inch pieces

4 garlic cloves, smashed

2 chiles in adobo sauce,
    with 2 teaspoons sauce

1 jalapeño pepper, halved

Zest and juice of 1 lime

Juice of 1 orange

1. In the slow cooker, mix the beef, garlic, chiles, jalapeño, lime zest and juice, and orange juice.

2. Cover and cook on Low for 6 to 8 hours. Discard the jalapeño before serving.

Nutritional Highlight: If you're enjoying a low-carb or paleo-style diet, skip the corn tortillas in favor of lettuce leaves.

Nutritional Information per Serving: Calories: 322; Fat: 11g; Protein: 52g; Carbohydrates: 1g; Sugar: 0g; Sodium: 113mg

Five-Spice Chili

GLUTEN-FREE **PALEO-FRIENDLY**

SERVES 4 TO 6

PREP TIME: 10 MINUTES • COOK TIME: 8 TO 10 HOURS ON LOW

A blend of spices delivers big flavor in this beef chili. Don't worry—the list looks long, but you probably already have most of the spices in your pantry. Chili is often served with cheese and corn chips, but this chili is so flavorful, you may find that a few slices of avocado and a sprinkle of cilantro leaves is all you need.

1 pound beef chuck

1 (28-ounce) can diced tomatoes,
   with juice

1 green pepper, diced

1 yellow or red pepper, diced

1 onion, diced

3 garlic cloves, minced

1 tablespoon ground cumin

1 teaspoon smoked paprika

½ teaspoon curry powder

¼ teaspoon cayenne pepper

¼ teaspoon ground cinnamon

Sea salt

Freshly ground black pepper

1. In the slow cooker, mix the beef, tomatoes, green and yellow peppers, onion, garlic, and spices. Season with salt and pepper.

2. Cover and cook on Low for 8 to 10 hours.

Tip: If you can, use grass-fed beef for this dish: Its flavor is significantly better, and it's lower in fat than conventionally farmed beef.

Nutritional Information per Serving: Calories: 285; Fat: 8g; Protein: 38g; Carbohydrates: 16g; Sugar: 8g; Sodium: 148mg

Beef and Squash Goulash with Pumpkin Seeds

GLUTEN-FREE

SERVES 4

PREP TIME: 5 MINUTES • COOK TIME: 8 HOURS ON LOW

This soul warming stew is full of iron, B-vitamins, omega-3s, and healthy anti-oxidants to keep winter colds and flu at bay. Serve it with a thick slice of whole grain bread and a crispy salad.

2 tablespoons tomato paste

1 cup beef broth

3 diced celery stalks

1 cup diced onion

4 carrots, peeled and sliced horizontally into "coins"

3 peeled and diced potatoes, about ½ pound

1 pound winter squash, peeled and diced

1½ pounds of beef chuck, cut in chunks for stew

4 cloves of garlic, peeled and chopped

1 teaspoon dried thyme

½ teaspoon rosemary

¼ teaspoon roast cinnamon

¼ teaspoon chipotle powder, optional

1 bay leaf

¼ cup pumpkin seeds

1. Whisk the tomato paste and beef broth until smooth, then set aside.

2. Add the remaining ingredients, except pumpkin seeds, to the slow cooker in the order given.

3. Pour the broth mixture over the top.

4. Cook on low for 8 to 10 hours.

5. Ladle into bowls and sprinkle with pumpkin seeds.

Nutritional Highlight: Not only is this dish high in iron and those important B vitamins but it packs a nutritional punch in each tiny pumpkin seed. One tablespoon of pumpkin seeds boots your immune system, gives you a kick of omega-3s, and increases the good LDL cholesterol.

Nutritional Information per Serving: Calories: 508; Fat: 15g; Protein: 58g; Carbohydrates: 34g; Sugar:6g; Sodium: 373mg

Meatballs in Marinara Sauce

SERVES 6 TO 8

PREP TIME: 15 MINUTES • COOK TIME: 2 HOURS ON HIGH

The best meatballs use a combination of ground meats for best flavor and perfect fat-to-protein ratio. Combining lean meat with bread crumbs soaked in milk keeps these meatballs moist and tender with less fat than traditional recipes.

½ cup stale bread crumbs

½ cup milk

1 pound lean ground beef

½ pound lean ground pork

½ pound ground veal

2 eggs, whisked thoroughly

1 teaspoon dried oregano

Sea salt

Freshly ground black pepper

1 tablespoon olive oil

8 cups prepared marinara sauce or
   Basic Marinara Sauce (page 186)

1 cup shredded mozzarella cheese

1. In a small bowl, mix the bread crumbs and milk. Set aside.

2. In a medium bowl, mix the ground meats, eggs, and oregano. Season with salt and pepper.

3. Squeeze the excess milk from the bread crumbs (discard milk). Add the soaked crumbs to the meat mixture and, using your hands, mix thoroughly. Using your hands, form the meat mixture into large balls about 2 to 3 inches in diameter each.

4. In a large skillet over medium heat, heat the oil. Cook the meatballs until browned on all sides. (They will not be completely cooked through.) Transfer the prepared meatballs to the slow cooker. Pour in the marinara sauce. Top with the shredded cheese.

5. Cover and cook on High for 2 hours, or until the meatballs are cooked through and the cheese is melted.

Tip: If desired, substitute ground pork for the veal.

Nutritional Information per Serving: Calories: 517; Fat: 18g; Protein: 54g; Carbohydrates: 20g; Sugar: 13g; Sodium: 1,052mg

THE HEALTHY SLOW COOKER COOKBOOK

Greek Meatballs

GLUTEN-FREE

SERVES 4 TO 6

PREP TIME: 10 MINUTES • COOK TIME: 6 HOURS ON LOW

Bring the flavors of the Mediterranean to your table with these simple, herb-infused Greek meatballs. Serve with whole-grain pita bread and a cool tzatziki sauce. Or, for a low-carb version, ditch the bread and wrap in butter lettuce leaves.

1 pound ground beef

½ cup cooked brown rice

½ cup finely chopped onion

1 teaspoon minced garlic

2 tablespoons finely chopped
fresh parsley leaves

1 teaspoon finely chopped
fresh mint leaves

1 teaspoon finely chopped fresh
oregano leaves

Sea salt

Freshly ground black pepper

1 egg, whisked

4 cups beef broth

1 (15-ounce) can plum tomatoes,
with juice

1. In a medium bowl, mix the beef, rice, onion, garlic, and herbs. Season generously with salt and pepper. Add the egg and, using your hands, mix thoroughly.

2. Form the meat mixture into balls 1 to 2 inches in diameter. Transfer them to the slow cooker. Gently pour in the broth and tomatoes.

3. Cover and cook on Low for 6 hours.

Tip: To save time, use bottled minced garlic. Its flavor is imperceptibly different from fresh garlic in cooked dishes.

Nutritional Information per Serving: Calories: 342; Fat: 10g; Protein: 43g; Carbohydrates: 17g; Sugar: 6g; Sodium: 927mg

Beef Stroganoff

SERVES 4 TO 6

PREP TIME: 5 MINUTES • COOK TIME: 8 HOURS ON LOW

In one meal, this American classic can easily sneak a day's worth of saturated fat and sodium right under your nose. But this version finds flavor in fresh herbs and quality meat without resorting to a can of condensed soup. Serve with egg noodles or on its own for a low-carb meal.

1 pound stewing beef, cut into
   1-inch chunks

1 cup beef broth

2 cups sliced mushrooms

¼ cup roughly chopped
   fresh parsley leaves

2 garlic cloves, minced

1 onion, diced

1 tablespoon Dijon mustard

Sea salt

Freshly ground black pepper

1 cup full-fat sour cream

1. In the slow cooker, mix the beef, broth, mushrooms, parsley, garlic, onion, and mustard. Season with salt and pepper.

2. Cover and cook on Low for 8 hours.

3. Uncover and let rest for 5 to 10 minutes before stirring in the sour cream. Taste and adjust seasonings.

Tip: The fat in sour cream is part of what stabilizes it when it is heated. Although low-fat sour cream may be used, it should be added when the beef mixture is at or below 140°F to prevent it from curdling.

Nutritional Information per Serving: Calories: 369; Fat: 20g; Protein: 39g; Carbohydrates: 7g; Sugar: 2g; Sodium: 403mg

Spicy Asian Beef

GLUTEN-FREE

SERVES 4

PREP TIME: 10 MINUTES • COOK TIME: 6 TO 8 HOURS ON LOW

If you're following a low-carb diet, skip the rice noodles and use bean sprouts or make your own "noodles" from carrots using a vegetable peeler or spiralizer to create long, wide strips.

1 pound beef steak, thinly sliced
   on a bias

1 tablespoon minced fresh ginger

1 teaspoon minced garlic

1 teaspoon Chinese five-spice powder

¼ cup orange juice

2 tablespoons lime juice

¼ teaspoon sea salt

Freshly ground black pepper

2 cups prepared rice noodles,
   for serving (optional)

1 cup shredded red cabbage,
   for serving

Crushed unsalted roasted peanuts,
   for serving

Fresh cilantro leaves, for serving

1. In the slow cooker, mix the beef, ginger, garlic, five-spice powder, orange juice, lime juice, and salt.

2. Cover and cook on Low for 6 to 8 hours. Taste and adjust seasonings with additional salt and pepper.

3. Serve over noodles (if using), accompanied with red cabbage, peanuts, and cilantro. For a lower-carb option, omit the noodles and double up on the cabbage.

Tip: The easiest way to cut beef on a bias is to freeze it first for about 30 minutes and then use a very sharp chef's knife or mandoline to slice it.

Nutritional Information per Serving: Calories: 324; Fat: 7g; Protein: 36g; Carbohydrates: 26g; Sugar: 2g; Sodium: 212mg

Shepherd's Pie

SERVES 4 TO 6

PREP TIME: 15 MINUTES • COOK TIME: 2 HOURS ON HIGH OR 6 TO 8 HOURS ON LOW

Is there anything quite as nostalgic as shepherd's pie? Not only is it a comfort food, but it's also pretty good for you, with carrots, onions, peas, and potatoes forming the backbone of the dish. If you're not a fan of lamb, simply use lean ground beef instead.

1 tablespoon olive oil

1 onion, diced

2 or 3 carrots, diced

1 pound ground lamb

1 cup frozen peas, thawed

Freshly ground black pepper

8 cups prepared mashed potatoes

½ cup sharp Cheddar

1. In a large skillet over medium heat, heat the oil. Add the onion and carrots and cook for 8 to 10 minutes, until softened. Push the vegetables to the side of the pan and increase the heat to medium-high. Add the lamb and cook until well browned. (If you wish to drain any of the fat, do so now.) Stir in the peas. Season with salt and pepper.

2. Transfer the mixture to the slow cooker. Top with the mashed potatoes, then sprinkle with the cheese.

3. Cover and cook on High for 2 hours or on Low for 6 to 8 hours.

Nutritional Highlight: Lamb is a terrific source of protein and is rich in several key vitamins and minerals, including vitamin B_{12}, niacin, zinc, selenium, iron, and riboflavin.

Nutritional Information per Serving: Calories: 799; Fat: 32g; Protein: 44g; Carbohydrates: 82g; Sugar: 11g; Sodium: 1,512mg

Roasted Garlic Rosemary Lamb with Lemon Potatoes

GLUTEN-FREE **PALEO-FRIENDLY**

SERVES 6 TO 8

PREP TIME: 10 MINUTES • COOK TIME: 6 TO 8 HOURS ON LOW

Garlic and rosemary are classically paired with lamb in this easy one-dish meal. A simple side salad or steamed vegetables is all you need to complete this dish.

6 garlic cloves, minced

1 tablespoon minced fresh rosemary

¼ teaspoon kosher salt

¼ teaspoon freshly ground black pepper

2 to 3 pounds boneless leg of lamb, trimmed

2 pounds small yellow potatoes

2 tablespoons olive oil

Zest and juice of 1 lemon

½ cup white wine or chicken broth

1. Using a mortar and pestle, grind the garlic, rosemary, salt, and pepper to a rough paste. (If you don't have a mortar and pestle, use a small bowl and the back of a fork or put the mixture in a small food processor to blend into a thick paste.) Spread all over the lamb leg and set aside.

2. In the slow cooker, mix the potatoes, oil, and lemon zest and juice until thoroughly coated. Pour in the wine. Put the prepared lamb leg on top of the potatoes.

3. Cover and cook on Low for 6 to 8 hours.

Tip: To increase the flavor, marinate the lamb in the herb and garlic rub for an hour (refrigerated) before cooking.

Nutritional Information per Serving: Calories: 450; Fat: 16g; Protein: 46g; Carbohydrates: 26g; Sugar: 2g; Sodium: 223mg

Herbed Lamb Chops

GLUTEN-FREE **PALEO-FRIENDLY**

SERVES 4 TO 6

PREP TIME: 10 MINUTES • COOK TIME: 6 HOURS ON LOW

Mint and parsley are traditional pairings with lamb. If you want to highlight the flavors even more, consider making a yogurt sauce with plain yogurt, finely chopped cucumber, and additional minced fresh mint and parsley leaves. Serve on the side or drizzle over each lamb chop.

1 tablespoon chopped fresh mint leaves

1 tablespoon chopped fresh
   parsley leaves

½ teaspoon sea salt

½ teaspoon freshly ground black pepper

¼ cup olive oil, divided

8 lamb loin chops (about 1½ to 2 pounds)

1 onion, thinly sliced

1. In a bowl, mix the mint, parsley, salt, and pepper with 2 tablespoons of oil. Spread the mixture over the lamb chops.

2. In the slow cooker, mix the onion and remaining 2 tablespoons oil. Put the herbed lamb chops over the onions.

3. Cover and cook on Low for 6 hours, or until the lamb is tender.

Tip: When you're cooking with olive oil, it's not necessary to use the most expensive, cold-pressed oil. Much of the flavor and nutrients are lost during the cooking process. Instead, use a virgin or light olive oil and save the extra-virgin, single-origin oils for salad dressings or drizzling over cooked vegetables.

Nutritional Information per Serving: Calories: 543; Fat: 29g; Protein: 64g; Carbohydrates: 3g; Sugar: 1g; Sodium: 407mg

Braised Lamb Shanks

GLUTEN-FREE **PALEO-FRIENDLY**

SERVES 4

PREP TIME: 10 MINUTES • COOK TIME: 8 TO 10 HOURS ON LOW

Serve these lamb shanks with egg noodles or mashed potatoes. They make an especially delicious holiday dinner.

4 (3-ounce) lamb shanks

2 cups full-bodied red wine

2 cups beef broth

2 tablespoons tomato paste

1 tablespoon olive oil

2 carrots, diced

2 stalks celery, diced

1 onion, diced

4 garlic cloves

4 fresh thyme sprigs

2 fresh rosemary sprigs

Sea salt

Freshly ground black pepper

1. In the slow cooker, mix the lamb, wine, broth, tomato paste, oil, carrots, celery, onion, garlic, thyme, and rosemary. Season with salt and pepper.

2. Cover and cook on Low for 8 to 10 hours.

Tip: To further develop the flavors of this dish, pan-sear the lamb shanks on all sides before putting them in the slow cooker. Browning creates a rich flavor that will permeate the entire dish.

Nutritional Information per Serving: Calories: 342; Fat: 11g; Protein: 27g; Carbohydrates: 12g; Sugar: 5g; Sodium: 547mg

Lamb Tagine

GLUTEN-FREE **PALEO-FRIENDLY**

SERVES 4 TO 6

PREP TIME: 10 MINUTES • COOK TIME: 6 TO 8 HOURS ON LOW

The dish is named after the Moroccan earthenware vessel it is usually cooked in. Fortunately, the slow cooker mimics the effects of cooking in a tagine—both are designed to capture condensation and retain moisture within the dish.

1 teaspoon ground turmeric

1 teaspoon ground ginger

1 teaspoon ground cinnamon

1 teaspoon smoked paprika

2 pounds lamb shoulder, cut into
   1-inch chunks

2 tablespoons olive oil, divided

2 onions, diced

1 cup raisins

Sea salt

Freshly ground black pepper

½ cup fresh cilantro leaves, for serving

1. In a small bowl, mix the turmeric, ginger, cinnamon, and paprika.

2. In a large bowl, toss the lamb with 1 tablespoon of the oil. Add the prepared spice mixture and toss again to coat.

3. Transfer the lamb to the slow cooker. Stir in the onions, raisins, and remaining 1 tablespoon of oil. Season generously with salt and pepper.

4. Cover and cook on Low for 6 to 8 hours. Serve garnished with cilantro leaves.

Nutritional Highlight: Spices such as ginger, turmeric, cinnamon, and paprika do more than simply flavor a dish—they're packed with health-protective antioxidants and phytochemicals. Turmeric may support your liver and digestive functions, cinnamon may lower LDL (or "bad" cholesterol), and ginger has anti-inflammatory effects.

Nutritional Information per Serving: Calories: 621; Fat: 24g; Protein: 65g; Carbohydrates: 35g; Sugar: 24g; Sodium: 236mg

Greek Lamb Stew

GLUTEN-FREE **PALEO-FRIENDLY**

SERVES 6 TO 8

PREP TIME: 5 MINUTES • COOK TIME: 6 TO 8 HOURS ON LOW

This lamb stew is delicious on its own or served as a filling for whole-grain pita bread, topped with crumbled feta cheese and diced cucumber.

3 pounds lamb shoulder, cut into 1-inch chunks

4 cups beef broth

1 (28-ounce) can plum tomatoes, with juice

2 cups white wine

6 garlic cloves, roughly chopped

2 onions, diced

1 tablespoon fresh oregano leaves or 1 teaspoon dried oregano

1 teaspoon fresh thyme leaves or ½ teaspoon dried thyme

1 bay leaf

Sea salt

Freshly ground black pepper

1. In the slow cooker, mix the lamb, broth, tomatoes, wine, garlic, onions, oregano, thyme, and bay leaf. Season with salt and pepper.

2. Cover and cook on Low for 6 to 8 hours. Discard the bay leaf before serving.

Tip: When cooking with wine, choose inexpensive bottles that you would enjoy drinking. The flavor will intensify as it cooks. In general, dry wines work better than sweet wines, whose sweetness becomes concentrated with cooking. Avoid what is sold as "cooking wine," which is more expensive per ounce than an inexpensive bottle of table wine and is loaded with sodium. If you prefer to cook without alcohol, substitute water or broth.

Nutritional Information per Serving: Calories: 564; Fat: 18g; Protein: 69g; Carbohydrates: 14g; Sugar: 8g; Sodium: 742mg

Roasted Lamb with Mustard and Fennel

GLUTEN-FREE **PALEO-FRIENDLY**

SERVES 6

PREP TIME: 10 MINUTES • COOK TIME: 6 TO 8 HOURS ON LOW

The sweet flavors of fennel intensify with long, slow cooking in wine and oil. Serve this dish with crusty bread to sop up all the delicious broth.

2 tablespoons olive oil, divided

1 teaspoon grainy mustard

1 teaspoon fennel seeds, crushed

Sea salt

Freshly ground black pepper

1 boneless leg of lamb (about 2 to 3 pounds)

1 fennel bulb, cored and thinly sliced

2 garlic cloves, minced

½ cup white wine

1. In a small bowl, mix 1 tablespoon of oil with the mustard and fennel seeds. Season with salt and pepper. Rub all over the lamb.

2. In the slow cooker, mix the fennel, garlic, remaining 1 tablespoon of oil, and wine. Put the lamb on top.

3. Cover and cook on Low for 6 to 8 hours, or until the lamb is tender.

Variation: If you're not a fan of mustard, mince an additional clove of garlic and add it to the rub mixture.

Nutritional Information per Serving: Calories: 494; Fat: 22g; Protein: 64g; Carbohydrates: 4g; Sugar: 0g; Sodium: 237mg

Moussaka

SERVES 6

PREP TIME: 20 MINUTES • COOK TIME: 6 TO 8 HOURS ON LOW

This recipe requires a bit more preparation, but the results are well worth the effort. Bonus: It's a one-dish meal, and a simple side salad is all you need to complete it.

1 eggplant, cut lengthwise into ¼-inch-thick slices

Sea salt

2 tablespoons olive oil

1 onion, diced

1 pound ground lamb

1 (15-ounce) can diced tomatoes, with juice

1 (10-ounce) jar roasted red peppers, drained and diced

1 tablespoon minced garlic

1 teaspoon ground cinnamon

1 teaspoon dried oregano

Freshly ground black pepper

1 tablespoon butter

1 tablespoon all-purpose flour

1 cup milk

1. Sprinkle the eggplant generously with salt and put in a colander for 15 minutes to drain. Rinse under cool running water. Using your hands, squeeze out excess liquid.

2. Meanwhile, in a large skillet over medium heat, heat the olive oil. Add the onion and cook for about 5 minutes, until softened. Add the ground lamb and cook until well browned. Stir in the tomatoes, roasted red peppers, garlic, cinnamon, and oregano. Season with salt and pepper.

3. While the onions and lamb are cooking; in a small saucepan, melt the butter. Whisk in the flour to form a paste. Add the milk and cook, whisking continuously, until thickened. Remove from the heat. Season with salt and pepper.

4. Line the bottom of the slow cooker with the eggplant. Top with the lamb and onion mixture. Pour in the milk mixture.

5. Cover and cook on Low for 6 to 8 hours.

Variation: For an extra-rich version of this dish, stir 6 ounces of crumbled feta cheese into the thickened milk mixture.

Nutritional Information per Serving: Calories: 278; Fat: 13g; Protein: 25g; Carbohydrates: 16g; Sugar: 9g; Sodium: 247mg

Sweets and Treats

Cinnamon Apple Pie Filling

GLUTEN-FREE **VEGETARIAN**

SERVES 10

PREP TIME: 15 MINUTES • COOK TIME: 6 TO 8 HOURS ON LOW

You can use this sweet filling to make a pie, but it's also delicious served over ice cream or topped with a small dollop of whipped cream.

4 pounds apples, peeled, cored,
  and sliced
1 cup hard apple cider
¼ cup coconut palm sugar
1 tablespoon butter

1 tablespoon ground cinnamon
¼ teaspoon ground nutmeg
¼ teaspoon sea salt
⅛ teaspoon ground allspice

1. In the slow cooker, mix the apples, cider, sugar, butter, cinnamon, nutmeg, salt, and allspice.

2. Cover and cook on Low for 6 to 8 hours, or until the apples are tender and fragrant.

3. Let cool for 30 minutes before serving.

Tip: Some apples hold their shape better than others when cooked. Red Delicious, McIntosh, and Braeburn apples tend to break down when cooked, whereas Granny Smith, Royal Gala, Cortland, and Golden Delicious hold their shape.

Nutritional Information per Serving: Calories: 136; Fat: 1g; Protein: 0g; Carbohydrates: 33g; Sugar: 25g; Sodium: 68mg

THE HEALTHY SLOW COOKER COOKBOOK

Blueberry Pie Filling

GLUTEN-FREE **VEGETARIAN**

SERVES 8

PREP TIME: 5 MINUTES • COOK TIME: 4 TO 6 HOURS ON LOW

In late August, a surplus of blueberries comes rolling in, which means it's time for blueberry pie. Better yet, this filling is particularly delicious as the top layer of a no-bake cheesecake.

2 pounds fresh blueberries

¼ cup granulated sugar

1 tablespoon cornstarch

Juice of 1 lemon

1 tablespoon butter

1. In the slow cooker, mix the blueberries, sugar, and cornstarch. Drizzle with the lemon juice. Dot with butter.

2. Cover and cook on Low for 4 to 6 hours, or until the mixture is thick and syrupy.

3. Let cool completely before serving.

Variation: If you're craving this delicious pie filling in the dead of winter, don't worry! You can just as easily use frozen blueberries, which were picked and processed at the peak of freshness. Simply increase the cooking time by 1 or 2 hours.

Nutritional Information per Serving: Calories: 105; Fat: 2g; Protein: 1g; Carbohydrates: 24g; Sugar: 18g; Sodium: 11mg

Dates Poached in Coffee and Cardamom

GLUTEN-FREE **VEGAN**

SERVES 8

PREP TIME: 5 MINUTES • COOK TIME: 1 HOUR ON LOW

For a Moroccan-inspired dessert, serve these poached dates over plain Greek yogurt.

16 ounces Medjool dates, pitted

2 cups hot brewed coffee

½ teaspoon ground cardamom

Pinch sea salt

1. In the slow cooker, mix the dates, coffee, cardamom, and salt.

2. Cover and cook on Low for 1 hour, just long enough to allow the flavors to meld.

3. Let cool to room temperature before serving.

Nutritional Highlight: Although dates contain a significant amount of natural sugars per serving, the sweetness is offset by their dietary fiber. Unlike refined sugar, dates are rich in vitamins, minerals, and antioxidants, including vitamin B_6 and magnesium.

Nutritional Information per Serving: Calories: 163; Fat: 0g; Protein: 2g; Carbohydrates: 43g; Sugar: 37g; Sodium: 32mg

Pears Poached in Spiced Wine

GLUTEN-FREE **VEGAN**

SERVES 4

PREP TIME: 5 MINUTES • COOK TIME: 4 TO 6 HOURS ON LOW

During the holiday season, instead of serving a heavy, high-carb dessert after dinner, try these spiced poached pears. They're warming, sophisticated, and oh-so-easy in the slow cooker.

1 (750 ml) bottle red wine, such as pinot
   noir or Shiraz

¼ cup brown sugar

1 orange, thinly sliced

4 (3-inch) cinnamon sticks

2 whole star anise pods

4 ripe pears, peeled and left whole

1. In the slow cooker, mix the wine, sugar, orange, cinnamon, and star anise.

2. Using a paring knife, slice the bottom off each pear to create a flat surface so they can stand upright. Put the pears in the slow cooker.

3. Cover and cook on Low for 4 to 6 hours, or until the pears are tender, fragrant, and a brilliant dark red.

Variation: To make a flavorful, sweet wine and pear butter, use half the amount of wine called for here and dice the pears before adding to the slow cooker. Once the mixture is cooked, purée it until smooth. Cool and refrigerate in an airtight container. It's delicious served with crackers and cheese.

Nutritional Information per Serving: Calories: 347; Fat: 0g; Protein: 2g; Carbohydrates: 53g; Sugar: 35g; Sodium: 13mg

Cinnamon Pecan–Stuffed Apples

GLUTEN-FREE **VEGETARIAN**

SERVES 4

PREP TIME: 10 MINUTES • COOK TIME: 4 TO 6 HOURS ON LOW

This recipe resembles an inside-out apple pie, but it is much lower in carbs and saturated fat given that the "crust" is merely walnuts, cinnamon, and just a hint of brown sugar.

½ cup pecans, roughly chopped

2 tablespoons brown sugar

1 teaspoon ground cinnamon

¼ teaspoon ground nutmeg

Pinch sea salt

4 apples, cored

2 teaspoons butter

½ cup apple cider

1. In a bowl, mix the pecans, sugar, cinnamon, nutmeg, and salt.

2. In the slow cooker, place the apples upright. (You may need to slice a little off the base to help them stand straight.) Gently stuff the apples with the sugar mixture. Dot the tops with about ½ teaspoon of butter each.

3. Gently pour the apple cider around the apples.

4. Cover and cook on Low for 4 to 6 hours, or until the apples are tender and fragrant.

Nutritional Highlight: Pecans are rich in plant sterols, which may improve blood cholesterol levels. They're also a good source of oleic acid, the same type of fat found in olives and avocado that has been shown to be heart healthy.

Nutritional Information per Serving: Calories: 170; Fat: 5g; Protein: 1g; Carbohydrates: 34g; Sugar: 27g; Sodium: 76mg

Pistachio–Stuffed Nectarines

GLUTEN-FREE **VEGETARIAN**

SERVES 4

PREP TIME: 10 MINUTES • COOK TIME: 2 TO 4 HOURS ON LOW

Crunchy pistachios and sweet nectarines are a match made in heaven. You'll find that this rich filling works equally well in other stone fruits, such as peaches and apricots.

¼ cup shelled pistachios

1 tablespoon coconut palm sugar
  or brown sugar

½ teaspoon ground nutmeg

2 tablespoons butter

2 nectarines, halved and pitted

¼ cup white wine or water

1. Using a clean spice grinder or small food processor, pulse the pistachios until they resemble sand.

2. In a bowl, mix the ground pistachios with the sugar and nutmeg. Add the butter and mash into a paste. Divide the pistachio filling among the nectarine halves.

3. Put the stuffed nectarines in the slow cooker. Gently pour the wine around them.

4. Cover and cook on Low for 2 to 4 hours, or until the fruit is tender.

5. Let rest for about 30 minutes before serving warm.

Nutritional Highlight: Pistachios are rich in fiber and polyphenols, a combination that may support gut health and the "good bacteria" that you want down there.

Nutritional Information per Serving: Calories: 149; Fat: 9g; Protein: 2g; Carbohydrates: 13g; Sugar: 9g; Sodium: 46mg

Rice Pudding with Almonds

GLUTEN-FREE **VEGAN**

SERVES 8

PREP TIME: 5 MINUTES • COOK TIME: 3 TO 4 HOURS ON LOW

This rich, creamy dessert boasts a surprising amount of nutrition due to the almonds and brown rice. Plus, it's completely vegan.

8 cups vanilla almond milk

2 cups brown jasmine rice

1 cup raisins

1 cup slivered almonds

1 tablespoon ground cinnamon

Pinch sea salt

1. In the slow cooker, mix the almond milk, rice, raisins, almonds, cinnamon, and salt.

2. Cover and cook on Low for 3 to 4 hours, or until the rice is tender.

Nutritional Highlight: Just 1 cup of cooked brown rice supplies nearly 100 percent of your daily value of manganese, which plays an important role in bone development and metabolism. The whole grain is also rich in selenium, phosphorus, copper, magnesium, and vitamin B_3.

Nutritional Information per Serving: Calories: 325; Fat: 11g; Protein: 8g; Carbohydrates: 51g; Sugar: 11g; Sodium: 193mg

Mixed Berry Crisp

VEGAN

SERVES 8

PREP TIME: 10 MINUTES • COOK TIME: 1 TO 2 HOURS ON HIGH

You may not believe that this sweet treat is as healthy as granola and berries. Serve it guilt-free—it won't send your blood sugar skyrocketing.

¼ cup whole wheat pastry flour

¼ cup old-fashioned rolled oats

¼ teaspoon sea salt

2 tablespoons coconut palm sugar

1 teaspoon pure vanilla extract

4 tablespoons coconut oil, divided

2 cups fresh blueberries

2 cups fresh blackberries

1 cup fresh strawberries, hulled
   and halved

1 tablespoon cornstarch

1. In a mixing bowl, mix the flour, oats, salt, and sugar. Using the back of a fork, mix in the vanilla and all but 1 teaspoon of the oil.

2. Grease the inside of the slow cooker crock with the remaining oil.

3. Put the berries in the slow cooker and sprinkle with the cornstarch. Stir gently to combine. Spread the oat mixture evenly over the top.

4. Cover and cook on High for 1 to 2 hours. Let rest for at least 15 minutes before serving.

Nutritional Highlight: Berries are a rich source of antioxidants, especially blackberries and blueberries. They also contain a generous dose of fiber and have very little sugar compared with other fruits.

Nutritional Information per Serving: Calories: 143; Fat: 7g; Protein: 2g; Carbohydrates: 19g; Sugar: 9g; Sodium: 66mg

Plum Cobbler

VEGETARIAN

SERVES 8

PREP TIME: 10 MINUTES • COOK TIME: 3 TO 4 HOURS ON HIGH

Cobbler is a classic summertime dessert. Tart yet sweet plums are married with honey to create a deliciously syrupy sauce for the biscuit topping.

2 pounds plums, pitted and diced

½ cup liquid honey

1 teaspoon ground cinnamon

1 cup whole wheat biscuit mix

1 cup milk

2 tablespoons brown sugar

1. In the slow cooker, mix the plums, honey, and cinnamon.

2. In a medium mixing bowl, stir the biscuit mix, milk, and sugar. Spoon the dough over the plums.

3. Cover and cook on High for 3 to 4 hours.

Nutritional Highlight: One fresh plum supplies nearly 10 percent of your daily value of vitamin C. Plums are also a good source of fiber, vitamin K, copper, and potassium. Plums vary widely in their sweetness, so adjust the amount of honey you use in this recipe accordingly.

Nutritional Information per Serving: Calories: 172; Fat: 1g; Protein: 3g; Carbohydrates: 40g; Sugar: 29g; Sodium: 183mg

Blackberry Rosemary Cobbler

VEGETARIAN

SERVES 8

PREP TIME: 5 MINUTES • COOK TIME: 1 TO 2 HOURS ON HIGH

Blackberries are rich in anthocyanins, a phytonutrient that protects the brain from oxidative stress and may reduce age-related conditions such as Alzheimer's disease and dementia.

6 cups fresh blackberries

1 teaspoon cornstarch

1 teaspoon minced fresh rosemary

1 cup whole wheat biscuit mix

1 cup milk

2 tablespoons granulated sugar

1. In the slow cooker, mix the blackberries, cornstarch, and rosemary.

2. In a medium mixing bowl, stir the biscuit mix, milk, and sugar. Spoon the dough over the blackberry mixture.

3. Cover and cook on High for 1 to 2 hours.

Variation: Fresh herbs bring a surprising and complex flavor to desserts. Experiment with other combinations, such as apples and thyme, peaches and tarragon, or blueberries and basil.

Nutritional Information per Serving: Calories: 124; Fat: 2g; Protein: 4g; Carbohydrates: 25g; Sugar: 10g; Sodium: 182mg

Spreads and Sauces

Ginger Pear Butter

GLUTEN-FREE **VEGAN** **PALEO-FRIENDLY**

MAKES 4 TO 6 CUPS, 32 SERVINGS

PREP TIME: 10 MINUTES • COOK TIME: 2 TO 4 HOURS ON LOW

Use this spicy sauce in an appetizer platter or to complement a dessert. It complements both sweet and savory dishes.

6 ripe pears, peeled, cored, and diced

1 cup water

1 teaspoon lime juice

1 teaspoon minced fresh ginger

1. In the slow cooker, mix the pears, water, lime juice, and ginger.

2. Cover and cook on Low for 2 to 4 hours.

3. Cool, cover, and refrigerate until ready to serve.

Nutritional Highlight: Pears contain flavonoids that may improve insulin sensitivity. They're also rich in fiber, copper, and vitamins C and K.

Nutritional Information per Serving: Calories: 23; Fat: 0g; Protein: 0g; Carbohydrates: 6g; Sugar: 4g; Sodium: 1mg

Blueberry Butter

GLUTEN-FREE **VEGAN** **PALEO-FRIENDLY**

MAKES 6 CUPS, 24 SERVINGS

PREP TIME: 5 MINUTES • COOK TIME: 2 TO 4 HOURS ON LOW

If you have more blueberries than you know what to do with, make this gorgeous blueberry spread. It's great on morning toast or as an accompaniment to roasted meats.

8 cups fresh blueberries
1 cup water

1 teaspoon pure vanilla extract

1. In the slow cooker, mix the blueberries, water, and vanilla. Using a wooden spoon, gently mash the blueberries to break their skins and release their juices.

2. Cover and cook on Low for 2 to 4 hours.

3. Cool, cover, and refrigerate until ready to use.

Nutritional Highlight: Blueberries are a rich source of antioxidants, which help neutralize cell-damaging free radicals. They're also a good source of fiber and have a low glycemic index, which means they offer a gradual source of energy.

Nutritional Information per Serving: Calories: 28; Fat: 0g; Protein: 0g; Carbohydrates: 7g; Sugar: 5g; Sodium: 1mg

Chunky Fig Spread

GLUTEN-FREE **VEGAN** **PALEO-FRIENDLY**

MAKES 3 TO 4 CUPS, 24 SERVINGS

PREP TIME: 5 MINUTES • COOK TIME: 4 TO 6 HOURS ON LOW

This flavorful spread is perfect on crackers or as a glaze for pork.

1 pound fresh figs, stemmed and halved

1½ cups water

2 tablespoons coconut palm sugar

1 lemon, juiced

1. In the slow cooker, mix the figs, water, and sugar.

2. Cover and cook on Low for 4 to 6 hours.

3. Stir in the lemon juice.

4. Cool, cover, and refrigerate until ready to serve.

Tip: If you prefer a smooth spread, simply purée the cooked figs using an immersion or stand blender.

Nutritional Information per Serving: Calories: 51; Fat: 0g; Protein: 1g; Carbohydrates: 13g; Sugar: 10g; Sodium: 5mg

Tomatillo Salsa

GLUTEN-FREE **VEGAN** **PALEO-FRIENDLY**

MAKES 6 TO 8 CUPS, 12 SERVINGS

PREP TIME: 10 MINUTES • COOK TIME: 8 HOURS ON LOW

If you're looking for authentic Mexican flavors, look no further than this slow-roasted tomatillo salsa.

1 pound tomatillos, husks removed

2 onions, cut into rings

4 garlic cloves, mashed

1 jalapeño pepper, halved lengthwise

1 cup water

Sea salt

Freshly ground black pepper

¼ cup lime juice

¼ cup minced fresh cilantro

1. Core the tomatillos and slice the larger ones in quarters and the smaller ones in half.

2. In the slow cooker, mix the tomatillos, onions, garlic, jalapeño, and water. Season with salt and pepper.

3. Cover and cook on Low for 8 hours.

4. Stir in the lime juice and cilantro.

5. If a smoother salsa is desired, purée using a stand or immersion blender.

Tip: The seeds are often thought to be the spiciest portion of a hot pepper, but did you know that the membranes actually pack the most heat? Thus, if you're looking to make this salsa milder, discard the seeds and membrane of the jalapeño.

Nutritional Information per Serving: Calories: 22; Fat: 0g; Protein: 1g; Carbohydrates: 4g; Sugar: 1g; Sodium: 21mg

Basic Marinara Sauce

GLUTEN-FREE VEGAN PALEO-FRIENDLY

MAKES 8 CUPS, 8 SERVINGS

PREP TIME: 5 MINUTES • COOK TIME: 4 TO 6 HOURS ON LOW

Use this tomato sauce as a base for lasagna or simply slather it over pizza or pasta for a quick weeknight meal. Unlike store-bought versions, this tomato sauce contains no added sugar or, worse yet, high-fructose corn syrup. When you start with good-quality ingredients, you just need to step aside and let them shine.

2 (28-ounce) cans whole plum tomatoes, with juice

¼ cup roughly chopped fresh basil leaves

2 garlic cloves, minced

1 large onion, diced

Sea salt

Freshly ground black pepper

1. In the slow cooker, mix the tomatoes, basil, garlic, and onion. Use the back of a spoon to break up the tomatoes. Season with salt and pepper.

2. Cover and cook on Low for 4 to 6 hours.

3. If desired, use a stand or immersion blender to purée the sauce.

4. Cool, cover, and refrigerate until you're ready to use it.

Tip: If fresh basil isn't in season, substitute 1 teaspoon dried basil or look for whole plum tomatoes stewed with fresh basil.

Nutritional Information per Serving: Calories: 59; Fat: 0g; Protein: 2g; Carbohydrates: 12g; Sugar: 6g; Sodium: 64mg

Vodka Cream Sauce

GLUTEN-FREE **VEGETARIAN**

SERVES 6 TO 8

PREP TIME: 10 MINUTES • COOK TIME: 4 TO 6 HOURS ON LOW

Virtually all the alcohol cooks out of this flavorful sauce. What's left is a rich, complex, and deliciously creamy sauce for pasta or for dipping bread. Just be sure to add the cream at the very last minute. (It doesn't need to be reduced.)

1 teaspoon butter

1 shallot, minced

2 garlic cloves, minced

Pinch red pepper flakes

1 cup vodka

2 (28-ounce) cans crushed tomatoes, with juice

Sea salt

Freshly ground black pepper

½ cup heavy or whipping (35%) cream

½ cup freshly grated Parmesan cheese

¼ cup minced fresh basil leaves

1. In a small saucepan over medium heat, melt the butter. Add the shallot, garlic, and red pepper flakes, and cook for about 2 minutes. Add the vodka and cook for about 5 minutes, or until reduced by about half.

2. Transfer vodka mixture to the slow cooker. Stir in the tomatoes. Season with salt and pepper.

3. Cover and cook on Low for 4 to 6 hours.

4. Just before serving, stir in the cream, Parmesan, and basil. Cook until just heated through and thickened.

Tip: This recipe already contains half the fat of most vodka sauce recipes, but if you're trying to cut calories, simply stir in a tablespoon of cream at a time until it reaches the desired level of creaminess. Sometimes all you need is the suggestion of decadence to make a meal feel luxuriously rich.

Nutritional Information per Serving: Calories: 265; Fat: 6g; Protein: 10g; Carbohydrates: 23g; Sugar: 15g; Sodium: 644mg

Bolognese Sauce

GLUTEN-FREE PALEO-FRIENDLY

SERVES 6

PREP TIME: 10 MINUTES • COOK TIME: 4 TO 6 HOURS ON LOW

For a delicious low-carb menu option, serve this rich, meaty sauce over zucchini noodles and top with a sprinkle of Parmesan cheese.

1 teaspoon olive oil

1 pound lean ground beef

1 (28-ounce) can crushed tomatoes, with juice

½ cup white wine

1 cup diced carrots

1 cup diced onions

1 cup diced celery

2 garlic cloves, minced

1 teaspoon dried Italian herb blend

Sea salt

Freshly ground black pepper

1. In a skillet over medium-high heat, heat the oil. Add the ground beef and cook until browned. (It will not be completely cooked through.)

2. Transfer the beef to the slow cooker. Add the tomatoes, wine, carrots, onions, celery, garlic, and herbs. Season with salt and pepper.

3. Cover and cook on Low for 4 to 6 hours.

Variation: For a lower-fat sauce, use ground turkey instead of beef. Just be sure to purchase lean ground turkey; some is a combination of light and dark meat and may contain as many calories as ground beef.

Nutritional Information per Serving: Calories: 237; Fat: 6g; Protein: 27g; Carbohydrates: 16g; Sugar: 10g; Sodium: 373mg

Smoky Barbecue Sauce

GLUTEN-FREE **VEGAN** **PALEO-FRIENDLY**

MAKES 6 CUPS, 24 SERVINGS
PREP TIME: 5 MINUTES • COOK TIME: 6 TO 8 HOURS ON LOW

Most commercially prepared barbecue sauce contains a long list of ingredients that often begin with water and sugar or high-fructose corn syrup. Making your own sauce gives you greater control not only in choosing healthier ingredients but also infusing the sauce with more complex and delicious flavors.

4 cups tomato ketchup

1 cup water

¼ cup red wine or sherry vinegar

¼ cup coconut palm sugar

1 onion, minced

2 garlic cloves, minced

1 tablespoon smoked paprika

1 teaspoon ground chipotle chile

1 teaspoon dry mustard

Sea salt

Freshly ground black pepper

1. In the slow cooker, mix the ketchup, water, vinegar, sugar, onion, garlic, paprika, chipotle chile, and dry mustard. Season with salt and pepper.

2. Cover and cook on Low for 6 to 8 hours.

3. Cool, cover, and refrigerate until ready to use.

Nutritional Highlight: Coconut palm sugar is an unrefined brown sugar derived from the tropical coconut palm tree flower. It has a slightly lower glycemic index than table sugar and retains many nutrients that would otherwise be stripped away during the refining process, including iron, zinc, calcium, and potassium. Nevertheless, it still contains 4 grams of sugar per teaspoon, so its slightly higher nutritional profile shouldn't be a license for indulgence.

Nutritional Information per Serving: Calories: 52; Fat: 0g; Protein: 1g; Carbohydrates: 13g; Sugar: 11g; Sodium: 462mg

Sweet and Sour Sauce

GLUTEN-FREE **VEGAN** **PALEO-FRIENDLY**

MAKES 6 TO 8 CUPS, 24 SERVINGS

PREP TIME: 10 MINUTES • COOK TIME: 4 TO 6 HOURS ON LOW

Many commercially prepared sweet and sour sauces are loaded with sugar, making them more suited to dessert than a main dish. This version uses pineapple juice to sweeten it—a much healthier option.

4 cups pineapple juice

¼ cup apple cider vinegar

2 tablespoons tomato ketchup

1 onion, diced

1 small green pepper, diced

1 tablespoon cornstarch

¼ cup water

Sea salt

1. In the slow cooker, mix the pineapple juice, vinegar, ketchup, onion, and green pepper.

2. Cover and cook on Low for 4 to 6 hours.

3. To thicken the sauce, dissolve the cornstarch in the water and pour into the slow cooker during the last few minutes of cooking. Cook until just thickened. Season with salt.

4. Cool, cover, and refrigerate until ready to serve.

Tip: You know that burning sensation you feel on your tongue after eating several slices of pineapple? Pineapple contains a protein-digesting enzyme called bromelain. In fact, it's so powerful that if you were to marinate pork in pineapple juice for an extended period of time, it would turn into a pile of mush. So, be careful when using pineapple as a marinade.

Nutritional Information per Serving: Calories: 28; Fat: 0g; Protein: 0g; Carbohydrates: 7g; Sugar: 5g; Sodium: 27mg

THE HEALTHY SLOW COOKER COOKBOOK

Spicy Ginger Stir-Fry Sauce

MAKES 4 CUPS, 8 SERVINGS

PREP TIME: 5 MINUTES • COOK TIME: 4 HOURS ON LOW

Use this flavorful sauce as a base for stir-fries or as a dip for spring rolls. If you're feeding children, be conservative with the chile and ginger—a little goes a long way.

2 cups beef broth

1 cup soy sauce

¼ cup hoisin sauce

2 tablespoons coconut palm sugar

1 teaspoon minced fresh ginger

1 teaspoon minced red chile

2 garlic cloves, minced

Juice of 1 lime

¼ cup water

1 tablespoon cornstarch

1. In the slow cooker, mix the broth, soy sauce, hoisin, sugar, ginger, chile, garlic, and lime juice.

2. Cover and cook on Low for 4 hours.

3. To thicken the sauce, dissolve the cornstarch in the water and pour into the slow cooker during the last few minutes of cooking. Cook until just thickened.

4. Cool, cover, and refrigerate until ready to use.

Variation: If you're making this sauce for a vegetarian meal, simply substitute vegetable broth for the beef broth.

Nutritional Information per Serving: Calories: 61; Fat: 1g; Protein: 4g; Carbohydrates: 11g; Sugar: 5g; Sodium: 2,124mg

The Dirty Dozen & Clean Fifteen

A nonprofit and environmental watchdog organization called Environmental Working Group (EWG) looks at data supplied by the US Department of Agriculture (USDA) and the Food and Drug Administration (FDA) about pesticide residues and compiles a list each year of the best and worst pesticide loads found in commercial crops. You can use these lists to decide which fruits and vegetables to buy organic to minimize your exposure to pesticides and which produce is considered safe enough to skip the organics. This does not mean they are pesticide-free, though, so wash these fruits and vegetables thoroughly.

These lists change every year, so make sure you look up the most recent before you fill your shopping cart. You'll find the most recent lists as well as a guide to pesticides in produce at EWG.org/FoodNews.

2014 DIRTY DOZEN

Apples

Celery

Cherry tomatoes

Cucumbers

Grapes

Nectarines (imported)

Peaches

Potatoes

Snap peas (imported)

Spinach

Strawberries

Sweet bell peppers

In addition to the dirty dozen, the EWG added two produce contaminated with highly toxic organophosphate insecticides:

Blueberries (domestic)

Hot peppers

2014 CLEAN FIFTEEN

Asparagus

Avocados

Cabbage

Cantaloupes (domestic)

Cauliflower

Eggplants

Grapefruits

Kiwis

Mangos

Onions

Papayas

Pineapples

Sweet corn

Sweet peas (frozen)

Sweet potatoes

Measurement Conversions

VOLUME EQUIVALENTS (LIQUID)

US STANDARD	US STANDARD (OUNCES)	METRIC (APPROXIMATE)
2 tablespoons	1 fl. oz.	30 mL
¼ cup	2 fl. oz.	60 mL
½ cup	4 fl. oz.	120 mL
1 cup	8 fl. oz.	240 mL
1½ cups	12 fl. oz.	355 mL
2 cups or 1 pint	16 fl. oz.	475 mL
4 cups or 1 quart	32 fl. oz.	1 L
1 gallon	128 fl. oz.	4 L

OVEN TEMPERATURES

FAHRENHEIT (F)	CELSIUS (C) (APPROXIMATE)
250	120
300	150
325	165
350	180
375	190
400	200
425	220
450	230

VOLUME EQUIVALENTS (DRY)

US STANDARD	METRIC (APPROXIMATE)
⅛ teaspoon	0.5 mL
¼ teaspoon	1 mL
½ teaspoon	2 mL
¾ teaspoon	4 mL
1 teaspoon	5 mL
1 tablespoon	15 mL
¼ cup	59 mL
⅓ cup	79 mL
½ cup	118 mL
⅔ cup	156 mL
¾ cup	177 mL
1 cup	235 mL
2 cups or 1 pint	475 mL
3 cups	700 mL
4 cups or 1 quart	1 L

WEIGHT EQUIVALENTS

US STANDARD	METRIC (APPROXIMATE)
½ ounce	15 g
1 ounce	30 g
2 ounces	60 g
4 ounces	115 g
8 ounces	225 g
12 ounces	340 g
16 ounces or 1 pound	455 g

References

■ ■

The Best of Gourmet 2006. New York: Condé Nast Books, 2006.

Cheskin, Lawrence Jay, MD, Lisa Michelle Davis, Andrea Hanlon Mitola, Thomas Lycan, Brooke Mickle, Vanessa Mitchell, Leah Lipsky, and Emily Adkins. "Caloric Compensation, Satiety, and Dietary Satisfaction When Meat Entrees Are Substituted with White Button Mushrooms." *Journal of the Federation of American Societies for Experimental Biology*, March 2007. www.fasebj.org/cgi/content/meeting_abstract/21/6/LB58-b

Environmental Working Group. "Executive Summary." Accessed June 21, 2014. www.ewg.org /foodnews/summary.php

Garza, Lisa. "Slow Cooked Savory Herbed Amaranth." Gluten Free Foodies. Accessed July 7, 2014. www.glutenfreefoodies.co/2013/11/24/slow-cooked-savory-herbed-amaranth/

Good, Phyllis. *Fix-It and Forget-It New Cookbook*. Intercourse, PA: Good Books, 2013.

Hlebowicz, Joanna, Gassan Darwiche, Ola Björgell, and Lars-Olof Almér. "Effect of Cinnamon on Postprandial Blood Glucose, Gastric Emptying, and Satiety in Healthy Subjects." *American Journal of Clinical Nutrition*, vol. 85 no. 6: 1552–1556 (June 2007). ajcn.nutrition.org/content /85/6/1552.full

Kresser, Chris, "The Nitrate and Nitrite Myth: Another Reason Not To Fear Bacon." Accessed June 24, 2014. chriskresser.com/the-nitrate-and-nitrite-myth-another-reason-not-to-fear-bacon

López-Alt, J. Kenji. "The Food Lab's Top Nine Tips for Perfect Apple Pie." Serious Eats. Accessed July 7, 2014. sweets.seriouseats.com/2012/11/food-lab-top-nine-tips-for-perfect-apple-pie.html

Mayo Clinic. "Nutrition and Healthy Eating." Accessed June 21, 2014. www.mayoclinic.org/ healthy-living/nutrition-and-healthy-eating/basics/healthy-diets/hlv-20049477

———. "Omega-3 in Fish: How Eating Fish Helps Your Heart." Accessed July 7, 2014. www. mayoclinic.org/diseases-conditions/heart-disease/in-depth/omega-3/art-20045614

Mercola, Dr. Joseph. "Bone Broth: One of Your Most Healing Diet Staples." Mercola.com, December 16, 2013. Accessed July 5, 2014. articles.mercola.com/sites/articles/archive/2013 /12/16/bone-broth-benefits.aspx

Monterey Bay Aquarium. "Seafood Watch; Prawn—Freshwater." Accessed July 7, 2014. www.seafoodwatch.org/cr/SeafoodWatch/web/sfw_factsheet.aspx?gid=58

Oregon State University, Linus Pauling Institute. Micronutrient Information Center: "Manganese." Accessed July 7, 2014. lpi.oregonstate.edu/infocenter/minerals/manganese/

Paniagua, J.A., A. Gallego de la Sacristana, I. Romero, A. Vidal-Puig, J.M. Latre, E. Sanchez, P. Perez-Martinez, J. Lopez-Miranda, and F. Perez-Jimenez. "Monounsaturated Fat-Rich Diet Prevents Central Body Fat Distribution and Decreases Postprandial Adiponectin Expression Induced by a Carbohydrate-Rich Diet in Insulin-Resistant Subjects." American Diabetes Association, *Diabetes Care*, July 2007. care.diabetesjournals.org/content/30/7/1717.full

Rappaport, Rachel. *The Big Book of Slow Cooker Recipes*. Avon, MA: Adams Media, 2013.

Scharf, Rebecca J., Ryan T. Demmer, Mark D. DeBoer. "Longitudinal Evaluation of Milk Type Consumed and Weight Status in Preschoolers." *Archives of Disease in Childhood*, March 18, 2013. adc.bmj.com/content/early/2013/02/13/archdischild-2012-302941.short?g=w_adc_ahead_tab

Sisson, Mark. "16 Things That Affect Your Gut Bacteria." Mark's Daily Apple. Accessed July 7, 2014. www.marksdailyapple.com/16-things-that-affect-your-gut-bacteria/#axzz36oceQNDB

———. "Alternatives to Grains?" Mark's Daily Apple. Accessed June 30, 2014. www.marksdailyapple.com/alternatives-to-grains-quinoa/#axzz36X5frf5Y

Torrens, Kerry. "The Health Benefits of … Nuts." BBC Good Food. Accessed July 7, 2014. www.bbcgoodfood.com/howto/guide/health-benefits-nuts

USDA. "Danger Zone." Accessed June 21, 2014. www.fsis.usda.gov/wps/portal/fsis/topics/food-safety-education/get-answers/food-safety-fact-sheets/safe-food-handling/danger-zone-40-f-140-f/ct_index

The World's Healthiest Foods. "Ginger." Accessed June 27, 2014. www.whfoods.com/genpage.php?tname=foodspice&dbid=72

The World's Healthiest Foods. "Pears." Accessed June 30, 2014. www.whfoods.com/genpage.php?tname=foodspice&dbid=28

Worthington, Virginia. "Nutritional Quality of Organic Versus Conventional Fruits, Vegetables, and Grains." *Journal of Alternative and Complementary Medicine*, April 2001, 7(2): 161–173. doi:10.1089/107555301750164244. http://online.liebertpub.com/doi/abs/10.1089/107555301750164244

Recipe Index

Index

■ ■ ■ ■ ■ ■ ■ ■ ■ ■ ■ ■ ■ ■ ■ ■ ■ ■ ■ ■

Index

CPSIA information can be obtained at www.ICGtesting.com
Printed in the USA
BVOW10s1732301215

431404BV00004B/11/P